EMBRACING
THE FEAR

ABOUT THE AUTHORS

JUDITH BEMIS, a recovered agoraphobic, holds a B.S. in Education from the University of Minnesota and did post-graduate work at Michigan State University in East Lansing. An educator for over twenty-five years, she has also worked as a consultant to Abbott-Northwestern Hospital's Behavioral Medicine Clinic in Minneapolis. She is founder and director of the Open Door, a network of support groups for people with agoraphobia and other anxiety disorders.

A. BARRADA is a recovered agoraphobic and a psychotherapist. He has a Ph.D. in English and Linguistics from the University of MInnesota. In the mid-seventies he suffered from a severe case of agoraphobia and for a while he was virtually housebound. After his recovery, his therapist hired him as an assistant, and for two years he worked with people suffering from phobias and obsessive-compulsive disorder. Since 1982 he has been employed by the Behavioral Medicine Clinic at Abbott-Northwestern Hospital in Minneapolis. In 1989 he began a Ph.D. program in Clinical Psychology at the Fielding Institute, earning his master's degree in Clinical Psychology from the Institute in June 1991.

EMBRACING THE FEAR

Learning to Manage Anxiety and Panic Attacks

Judith Bemis
Amr Barrada

Hazelden Educational Materials
Center City, Minnesota 55012-0176

Library of Congress Cataloging In Publication Data
Bemis, Judith.
    Embracing the fear: learning to manage anxiety and panic attacks
/ by Judith Bemis and Amr Barrada.
        p.   cm.
    Includes index.
    ISBN 0-89486-971-X : $10.00
    1. Fear 2. Anxiety. 3. Panic attacks. I. Barrada, Amr.
    II. Title.
    BF575.F2B37   1994
    616.85'223—dc20   94-131
                                                                        CIP

Editor's note

Hazelden Educational Materials offers a variety of information on chemical dependency and related areas. Our publications do not necessarily represent Hazelden's programs, nor do they officially speak for any Twelve Step organization.

All quotes and personal stories within this book are those of real men and women who have struggled with anxiety or panic disorders. Unless otherwise noted, all names and identifying details have been changed in order to protect the person's anonymity.

Note to the reader from the authors

This book is not meant to substitute for therapy for people with anxiety or panic disorders. We encourage readers to see these ideas as suggestions that we have found helpful, but not as instructions that must be followed without question. We also encourage readers who have had personal difficulty with anxiety to seek the help of a qualified therapist.

This book is printed in Goudy and Frutiger Light

A small child approached me one day clutching a bouquet of flowers.
"This is for my mother," she said, and I found myself wishing that I
could do the same.
And so, this is my bouquet of time, commitment, and caring,
dedicated in loving memory of my mother,
Dorothy Mae Faulkner.

—J.B.

To Mimi

—A.B.

CONTENTS

DEDICATION v
ACKNOWLEDGMENTS AND PREFACE viii
EPIGRAPH x

PART 1—THE PROBLEM: FEAR OF FEAR
  The Anxiety Disorders 3
  What Causes Anxiety Disorders? 5
  Anxiety Disorders and Alcohol 10
  Gaining a New Perspective 11
  What Is Recovery? 12

PART 2—THE SOLUTION: A COGNITIVE APPROACH
  Introduction to the Program 17
    Managing Our Anxiety 17
    Listening to Our Inner Dialogue 22
    Lifestyle Awareness 23

THE FOURTEEN STRATEGIES
  Strategy 1: Accepting Our Anxiety Disorder 26
  Strategy 2: Practicing a Self-Nurturing Inner Dialogue 31
  Strategy 3: Allowing the Sensations of Anxiety or Panic 36
  Strategy 4: Slowing Down 41
  Strategy 5: Letting Go of Control 46
  Strategy 6: Taking Risks 51
  Strategy 7: Allowing Catastrophic Thoughts 56
  Strategy 8: Learning and Talking About Our Anxiety Disorder 61
  Strategy 9: Keeping Our Expectations Low 66
  Strategy 10: Accepting Setbacks 70
  Strategy 11: Taking the Time Limit Out of Recovery 75
  Strategy 12: No Longer Anticipating Panic Attacks 79
  Strategy 13: Recognizing Our Inner Strength 84
  Strategy 14: Reaching Out to Others 88

PART 3—INTEGRATION: TAKING RISKS
  Putting the Program to Work 94
    Going to Church 96
    Going to the Dentist 98
    Going to the Supermarket 100
    Going to the Hair Salon 102
    Shopping at the Mall 104
    Going to a Restaurant 106
    Going to the Theater, Concerts, or Large Group Events 108
    Going to a Social Event or Party 111
    Going to Work, to a Conference, or on a Job Interview 114
    Driving Alone 117
    Riding on a Bus, in a Van, or in a Carpool 119
    Driving on the Expressway 121
    Taking a Trip 124
    Flying the Unfriendly Skies 127
  Conclusion 130

PART 4—APPENDIX
  Some Thoughts on Self-Care 135
  Organizing an Anxiety/Panic Support Group 140

BIBLIOGRAPHY AND SUGGESTED READING 146

INDEX 147

ACKNOWLEDGMENTS

I would like to thank my first teacher for teaching me the skills that helped change my life and made this book possible; the members of the Open Door, who have waited patiently for the completion of this book, for their part in the development of this program and for their many testimonials that appear in the following pages; and Al Bemis for his encouragement and support throughout the writing of this manuscript and for the countless number of times he assisted me at the computer   —J.B.

A number of authors have written on the subject of anxiety disorders, some of whom are listed in the Bibliography. Although some of the ideas in this book are original and are based on our own experiences, we would like to express our gratitude to those whose ideas have been an inspiration, have influenced our thinking, and may sometimes be reflected in the following pages: Aaron Beck, Dianne Chambless, Alan Goldstein, and the late Dr. Claire Weekes. We would like to thank our editor, Tim McIndoo, for believing in this book from the very beginning, for his persistence in getting it published, and for his sensitive and dedicated work on the manuscript.

—J.B. AND A.B.

PREFACE

There was a time when I (Judith Bemis) believed that I was the only person on earth who had ever experienced a panic attack. I had no idea what was happening to me, and in all my searching no one had any answers. It took eighteen years before anyone even gave it a name. Once I knew what I was dealing with, I was able to do something about my situation and move on with my life. As I gained insight and learned helpful coping strategies, I realized that I could live free of panic attacks.

Having moved beyond the boundaries of my own fear, I wanted to share my newfound freedom with others. In 1986 I founded the Open Door, a support group for people with agoraphobia and other anxiety disorders, and began to develop a program which would eventually become the essence of this book, *Embracing the Fear.*

I first met Amr Barrada in 1983. Amr had been working on and developing concepts that demonstrated a unique understanding of agoraphobia and other anxiety disorders. It was the first time that I had been introduced to the idea of giving oneself permission to have an anxiety or panic disorder without having to fix it. It was clear to me how this permissive attitude could lead to a more positive feeling about oneself, and could be essential to one's recovery.

Later, while working as a consultant at Abbott-Northwestern Hospital's Behavioral Medicine Clinic in Minneapolis, I asked Amr to collaborate with me on a self-help program, which would focus on this idea of acceptance and would include "inner dialogue," much of which originated in his paper entitled, "A and B Self-Talk: Alternative Coping Styles." I felt that his insight into the recovery process and the gentle tone of his B-talk would be of great value. Although this program was originally written to serve as a handbook for the Open Door, it was obvious to us that it would be helpful to anyone dealing with anxiety and panic attacks.

We know from experience that there is a way out of the panic–avoidance cycle. We know that a person does not have to live from day to day waiting for the next episode of panic to strike without warning. And we know that it is possible to break through the feeling of isolation that each panic sufferer experiences.

It is not the intent of this book to take the place of a good therapist, but to offer you support and to suggest ideas for dealing with anxiety, panic, and avoidance behavior. We want to suggest some insights into various personality traits so that you will gain a better understanding of yourself. And then we want to introduce you to an inner dialogue that can help you *embrace the fear.*

You are fortunate to be searching for answers at a time when anxiety and panic disorders are better understood. We know that these words cannot bring you the comfort you seek—what you are dealing with is not easy. Your suffering is intense. Most likely you are feeling isolated and alone. But take heart: this program offers more than insights and strategies—*Embracing the Fear* offers hope.

IT HELPS TO KNOW

It helps to know that we are not alone,
  that what we have has a name.

It helps to know that this is treatable,
  that we are not in danger,
and that we carry our safety within us.

It helps to know that this is only a feeling,
  and that this too shall pass.

PART 1

THE PROBLEM: FEAR OF FEAR

Oh, my God! What's happening to me? *I quickly got out of the car, hoping the fresh air would help.* Get a hold of yourself! You're going to be all right! *I reassured myself as I fought desperately to stay in control. I had never really thought much about dying. But standing there alone on that warm July morning, in the very prime of my life, I was suddenly faced with the thought that I could very well be dying. I was terrified!*

—JUDY

Imagine for a moment that you are driving down the freeway. Suddenly, for no apparent reason, your heart begins to race. Your breathing becomes labored. You find it difficult to swallow. Feeling light-headed, you grip the steering wheel and notice that your hands are perspiring. A feeling of panic washes over you. Your mind races as you try to grasp what is happening. You struggle to stay in control, but the harder you try, the more out of control you feel. You tell yourself, *Just stay calm!* But the panic continues to escalate. You try to distract yourself by listening to the car radio or focusing your attention on the traffic around you. Another wave of panic! Seconds pass like minutes. *What if I pass out? Maybe this is a heart attack!*

Terrified, overwhelmed with a sense of impending doom, you head for the nearest exit in a desperate attempt to get help. Once off the freeway, the feeling gradually subsides, leaving you shaken and bewildered.

This episode could have taken place in a shopping mall, a church, your favorite restaurant, or any number of other places. *You have experienced a panic attack.* The symptoms may vary, but the reaction is the same—terror!

Chances are, you associate the panic episode with the freeway and you begin to generalize: *If it happens on the freeway, it could happen elsewhere.* As you become more and more concerned about recurring panic attacks, your symptoms occur more frequently and you avoid more and more places until your world becomes very small. Eventually you may come to believe that the only safe place is within your own home. The nightmare has just begun. Helplessly caught up in a panic–avoidance cycle, you are now dealing with the phenomenon known as agoraphobia.

THE ANXIETY DISORDERS

Embracing the Fear encompasses five of the anxiety disorders recognized by the American Psychological Association: panic disorder with agoraphobia, panic disorder without agoraphobia, social phobia, simple phobia, and generalized anxiety disorder. Each of these is seen as a rather discrete problem, and each can be recognized by a set of more or less predictable characteristics.

Panic Disorder with Agoraphobia (PDA)

PDA, or simply agoraphobia, is the most common and most debilitating of the anxiety disorders. Many see it as a "fear of fear," or more specifically, a fear of being trapped and unable to get help. Those of us with PDA experience recurring panic attacks that seem to come from out of the blue. During a panic attack, some of the following symptoms can be present: increased heart rate; dizziness or lightheadedness; faintness; increased respiration; sweating; tension in the stomach, neck, or shoulders; trembling hands or legs; weak knees; shortness of breath; a feeling of suffocation; fatigue; difficulty swallowing; blurred vision; inability to concentrate; confusion; a feeling of unreality; a fear of dying; a fear of going crazy; or a sense of impending doom. Although the first episode often takes place in a specific situation, the time and place of subsequent episodes may be unpredictable. As a result, our lifestyle becomes very restricted. Feeling helpless and out of control, we are vulnerable to depression. PDA and depression often go hand in hand.

In order to feel safe or to protect ourselves from embarrassment, we avoid places where we think the unpredictable feelings of panic might occur. In extreme cases, this could mean quitting jobs and eventually becoming housebound. However, not all people who have agoraphobia become housebound. Many of us manage to white-knuckle it from day to day, cleverly concealing our fears from family and friends to avoid ridicule and to protect ourselves from further shame. The plight of the agoraphobic is frightening, lonely, and bewildering.

Panic Disorder without Agoraphobia

This problem is very similar to panic disorder *with* agoraphobia except that extensive avoidance does not take place. Also, fearful thoughts are usually limited to perceptions that our body is not functioning properly, that our health is unreliable, and that some sort of physical collapse may be imminent.

Social Phobia

Unlike agoraphobics, people with social phobia often experience the least anxiety when they are alone. They usually fear various situations which involve the presence of people. Bothersome situations include being in crowded public places, rooms, or vehicles; being in meetings, formal groups, or social gatherings; and giving a public presentation. Some common catastrophic thoughts include fears of becoming visibly anxious, being scrutinized closely and judged negatively, babbling or talking incoherently, and going through a severe breakdown during a public presentation. Social phobics may also experience panic attacks.

Simple Phobias

Those of us with simple phobias fear specific events or situations. Fears of specific animals or animal groups are among the most common. Also common is the fear of heights (acrophobia), which usually involves a fear of falling to one's death, or the fear of being hemmed in (claustrophobia), which can involve being in closed rooms, tunnels, airplanes, land vehicles, boats, elevators, and so on. Another set of phobias involves the fear of dying as a result of an automobile accident, drowning, or being struck by lightning.

Generalized Anxiety Disorder (GAD)

GAD involves persistent anxiety over a long period of time, with little respite. The intensity can sometimes stay high. Typically, those of us with GAD are stressed out about two or more major life problems (for example, work, personal finances, family, or illness). We feel that the problems are difficult to manage and that we have little control over them.

What Causes Anxiety Disorders?

Some researchers claim that people who experience recurring anxiety or panic attacks have a genetic predisposition to anxiety disorders. Other researchers see it as a behavioral problem. For some anxiety-panic sufferers, being told that their condition is hereditary gives them the feeling that they've just been given a life sentence. They see themselves as trapped in a situation over which they have no control, and they may give up trying to get well. Others feel a sense of relief, because seeing their problem as genetic frees them from shame.

Whatever the reason, the good news is that there is a way out of the anxiety or panic-avoidance cycle and, no matter how long we have suffered, it is possible for us to reach a point where the anxiety and panic are no longer troublesome. The approach of this book is decidedly cognitive. *Embracing the Fear* reassures us that we are still in charge of our lives, that there is something we can do about our anxiety and panic attacks, and that there is recovery.

The Role of the Environment

What kind of environment might predispose a person to an anxiety disorder? Perhaps we grew up with an overly critical parent or parent-figure whose high expectations gave us the feeling that we could do nothing right or that we were just not good enough. Or perhaps we had a parent who was overly protective, which gave us the message that we were living in an unsafe world and could not take care of ourselves. We might also have feared abandonment or rejection.

Many of us anxiety and panic sufferers come from dysfunctional families. We may have been victims of alcoholism and learned fear at an early age. As children, we continually lived on the edge, not knowing what to expect from one day to the next. Our world was not safe, nor was it controllable. Subjected to abuse, we felt helpless and demoralized. We developed unhelpful coping strategies, such as avoidance and repression of feelings, and felt a constant need to be on guard.

The Role of Stress

Many of us experienced significant levels of stress before experiencing major symptoms of anxiety. For some of us, stress built up over time until it reached a point where we could no longer cope. Those of us with anxiety problems have a style of coping with stressful events that persistently aggravates us. We make unreasonable demands on ourselves, telling ourselves that we have to cope well and that because these particular events do not bother anyone else, they shouldn't bother us. But the more we try not to let things bother us, the more we aggravate ourselves and the more stressful these events become.

Many of us who develop anxiety problems have experienced a death in the family, severe illness, the loss of a friend, separation from a loved one, divorce, relocation, or any of a number of similar events. Loss seems to be a major theme. The fear of separation or isolation can stem from early childhood; we may have experienced difficulties resulting from the disruption of affectional bonds, especially those with parents. A history of separation anxiety and a problem with dependency on others are not uncommon. We usually cannot distinguish between the loneliness we feel as the result of a personal loss and the loneliness or isolation we might feel driving on the freeway. Both can provoke anxiety or panic in us, but we fail to make the connection. We feel that the personal loss is understandable but tell ourselves that panic on the freeway is inexcusable.

The Role of Our Emotions

We typically do not accept our negative feelings. In fact, we seem to be unaccepting of all feelings, whether negative or positive. It is important to encourage ourselves to be permissive of our feelings, regardless of what they might be, since being out of touch with them contributes much to our anxiety. We have a very distinct style of interpreting our simplest thoughts and feelings—often seeing them as wrong, ridiculous, or irrational. We tell ourselves that we must be strong and that we must not give in to negative feelings, such as sadness, grief, or fear. The more unwilling we are to experience certain thoughts and feelings, the more we're troubled by them. We try hard to control them or get rid of them. But all this effort is exactly what gets us into trouble, since the need to control and get rid of them is the best recipe for continued aggravation and distress.

The Role of Our Self-Talk

Those of us with anxiety disorders have a style of *self-talk* that demeans and dehumanizes us. It is nonpermissive and shaming. For example, we might tell ourselves, *I shouldn't be feeling this way!* or, *This is ridiculous!* The more we use this kind of self-talk, the more distressed we become and the more likely we are to experience anxiety or panic. Not realizing that our self-talk is counterproductive, that it acts against us, we try even harder to use the only strategies we are familiar with: avoidance, distraction, and being overly intellectual and analytical. The harder we try, the worse things get for us; and the worse things get, the harder we try. We find ourselves locked into a seemingly endless cycle of self-talk and distress. We shall see later that there is an effective way out of this cycle.

The Role of Perfectionism

Perfectionism plays a large part in laying the groundwork for anxiety problems. We spend much of our lives telling ourselves that we can't accept failure or perceived inadequacies. We develop and insist on high expectations and often feel that we never do enough or that what we do is not good enough. We do not accept ourselves, our thoughts, or our feelings; we adopt all-or-nothing ways of thinking. All of this places heavy demands on us. We use the same perfectionistic strategies in dealing with our anxiety problem. They are very complex, and our motives for using them sound extremely logical.

There are five major perfectionistic strategies:

1. *Raising expectations.* These strategies compel us to generate very high expectations of doing well and are usually signaled by such expressions as *I must, I have to, I should, I've got to,* and *I can't.* Presumably, the higher our expectations, the better we will cope. For example: *I've got to go to the mall today! I just can't continue to avoid it anymore! And when I get there, I've got to do well! I can't allow myself to get anxious! I've got to control myself or else something awful might happen! I must never even think about escaping! That would be too shameful and unacceptable!* How can anyone do well under such extreme pressure? It is no wonder that even the simplest tasks become forbiddingly difficult.

2. *Absolutism.* These are all-or-nothing strategies. We presume that if we corner ourselves into a limited set of options, the "perfect" choice will be obvious. Therefore, our freedom of choice becomes highly restricted: *I've got to drive on the freeway*

today and do so *without any trouble! I must have no anxiety whatso-
ever! I've got to go where I'm going without taking the easiest route!*
With our choices so restricted it is no wonder that we often feel
trapped by our thoughts and cannot make decisions or engage
in problem solving.

3. *Acceleration.* Strategies of acceleration are based on the idea that
the best way to do anything is to do it as quickly as possible. It
doesn't matter if we fall flat on our face while doing it. We have
little appreciation of the fact that often the fastest way of completing a task is to do it slowly and with clarity of mind.

4. *Control.* These are strategies of trying to keep under control
feelings and catastrophic thoughts that are perceived to be
uncontrollable: *I can't let things get out of hand! If I do, then they
will get even more out of hand, and that would be humiliating!*

5. *Elimination.* Of the five, this strategy appears to be the most
pervasive. It involves using avoidance, distraction, prevention,
substitution, diversion, camouflage, denial, rationalization,
minimization, and other strategies to "get rid of" unwanted feelings, thoughts, and behaviors. Of course, feelings, thoughts, and
behaviors are not easily eliminated, and trying to do so merely
makes us more troubled by them.

Other Factors

Often we do not feel in charge of our lives. We feel helpless and do
not assert ourselves in our relationships; we fail to establish boundaries and express our needs. Our self-esteem often depends on how we
think other people judge us. To feel good about ourselves or to be
accepted, we constantly seek the approval of others. Our low self-
esteem and lack of self-confidence keep us from taking risks; we often
feel stuck.

In many cases, life has become a treadmill that is moving faster
than we can handle. Feeling pressured, we have a difficult time slowing down or taking time for ourselves. We continually tell ourselves
that we have to hurry through various tasks, even the simplest ones.
Is it any wonder that life has become unmanageable and that anxiety
and panic have become a way of life?

9

ANXIETY DISORDERS AND ALCOHOL

People suffering from anxiety disorders in general, and agoraphobia in particular, appear to use chemicals, especially alcohol, to relieve their symptoms. It may be that agoraphobia, in many cases, follows attempts to relieve anxiety symptoms.[1] One study found that as many as one-third of agoraphobics who are also alcoholics said they began drinking as a way of controlling their anxiety symptoms.[2]

In a 1990 article, Kushner and colleagues suggested that there is a reciprocal relation between anxiety and alcoholism. A person may begin with the belief that drinking alcohol can alleviate anxiety, which leads to actually drinking, which leads to increased anxiety, which leads to further alcohol consumption. It may be that the more anxious people become, the more alcohol they feel they need to consume to alleviate their anxiety. And this reinforces their belief that alcohol reduces anxiety.

Another study reports that between 10 and 40 percent of alcoholics have a panic-related anxiety disorder, and that about 10 to 20 percent of people suffering from an anxiety disorder abuse either alcohol or other drugs.[3] One interesting finding this study makes is that the majority of people who suffer from both alcoholism and an anxiety problem say that the anxiety problem came before the alcohol problem. A similar earlier study also found that anxiety disorders usually preceded alcoholism: 59 percent of the participants with anxiety disorders reported using alcohol as a means of coping with anxiety.[4] This stresses the primacy of anxiety in many cases of alcoholism.

From these and similar studies it is tempting to conclude that excessive use of alcohol and other substances has a harmful effect on anxiety-related problems.

---

1. M. G. Kushner, K. J. Sher, and B. D. Beitman, "The Relation Between Alcohol Problems and the Anxiety Disorders," *The American Journal of Psychiatry* 147 (1990): 685-695.
2. J. Bibb and D. L. Chambless, "Alcohol Use and Abuse Among Diagnosed Agoraphobics," *Behaviour Research and Therapy* 24 (1986): 49-58.
3. B. J. Cox, G. R. Norton, R. P. Swinson, and N. S. Endler, "Substance Abuse and Panic-Related Anxiety: A Critical Review," *Behaviour Research and Therapy* 28 (1990): 385-393.
4. D. L. Chambless, J. Cherney, G. C. Caputo, and B. J. G. Rheinstein, "Anxiety Disorders and Alcoholism: A Study with Inpatient Alcoholics," *Journal of Anxiety Disorders* 1 (1987): 29-40.

GAINING A NEW PERSPECTIVE

It is difficult for us to think that there's anything positive about an anxiety disorder. It feels so debilitating that we can perceive it only as an indication of abnormalcy and dysfunction. For example, agoraphobia is associated with a great deal of emotional, social, and occupational impairment. The quality of life of an agoraphobic person is by no means enviable.

From a different perspective, however, there is much about agoraphobia that is positive. First, anxiety is essentially a normal response to stress. Once this is accepted, even intense or persistent anxiety—and yes, even panic attacks—can be seen as serving a useful function in our lives (although we are unlikely to see this function when we are persistently being overwhelmed by anxiety). Can you imagine finding yourself in a life-threatening situation and not experiencing an intense anxiety reaction?

The usual response to this argument is that the fears of those who suffer from anxiety disorders are not experienced in life-threatening situations, that their fears are irrational and serve no useful function. Such is the perspective of someone suffering from agoraphobia. But let's look at it from another perspective. Agoraphobic fears have almost nothing to do with situations that are life-threatening; the situations do not pose a threat to our health or personal safety. A simple look at the kinds of situations that are typically feared by agoraphobics reveals that the threat posed is an *emotional* one; specifically, we feel threatened with a loss of self-esteem. When entering a feared situation, such as a shopping mall, most of our thoughts are focused on whether or not we will cope well—whether we will have uncomfortable feelings or "abnormal" thoughts, or engage in shameful behaviors that will compromise our self-esteem. The catastrophic thoughts of a typical agoraphobic (*What if I panic? What if I faint? What if I lose control and scream?*) essentially involve fears of loss of self-esteem. What we are really saying is *I had better not behave this way, for such behavior is disgraceful and humiliating.* Even thoughts of having a heart attack or a stroke, or of dying, can be related to our sense of self-worth, since being alive and healthy are inextricably linked with how we value ourselves.

The gist is that the shame-based quality of our fears can alert us to their usefulness, to the emotional meanings represented by our fears. For example, if we have a panic attack while shopping at a mall or driving on the freeway, our response may be one of extreme mystery: we see such reactions as meaningless or as signs of personal defectiveness. However, the panic attack can serve as an important signal to alert us that difficult issues in our lives are in pressing need of attention, and that perhaps the time has come to start taking risks to bring about important changes.

We hate our problem with a passion; we hate our fears, our avoidance behaviors, our catastrophic thoughts, and our dependency on other people to help us do the simplest things. The problem is so complex and causes so much grief that we are unlikely to see any merit in our fears and anxiety. However, as our journey in recovery begins and we start to make sense of what is happening to us, as we become more and more accepting of our problem, and as we learn to become more mobile and independent, the problem becomes less and less threatening and at some point can even be seen as a friend. In recovery, we often reach a point at which we are better off than we've ever been in our entire lives.

WHAT IS RECOVERY?

It is difficult for those of us who suffer from panic or chronic anxiety to believe that life could ever again be normal, especially if we have struggled with anxiety problems for a long time. But it *is* possible. The problem is that we often try to get better by using the same strategies that helped cause the problem: shaming ourselves, being intolerant of our thoughts and feelings, and trying hard to be perfect.

Typically, those of us who suffer from anxiety problems have extremely unrealistic expectations of ourselves. So it is natural for us to view our recovery with similar unrealistic expectations: we want a perfect recovery as soon as possible. The more perfect we insist our recovery should be, however, and the more we try to hurry it, the more disappointed we are likely to become in our efforts to get well.

Since anxiety problems become entrenched in our daily lives, and since our self-talk is an indelible part of how we think and how we cope with various aspects of our lives, it is likely that very little will change at first. Recovery takes time, and the more time we give ourselves, the more stable and long-lasting our recovery will be. Finding shortcuts seems like a good idea but usually leaves us open to more setbacks. James Kavanaugh, in his book *Search*, encourages his readers to "play the long game." If ever there were a need for playing the long game, it's in recovering from an anxiety disorder. But taking a long view of recovery will not be easy for us, since we already feel that life is passing us by.

When we develop a permissive attitude about our panic attacks, when we're able to let go of our fear of them, they lose their power and occur less and less often, until we no longer find ourselves waiting for that next wave of panic from out of the blue. As we gain more confidence and take more risks, we focus less and less on our anxiety and panic attacks. We no longer need to label ourselves "agoraphobic," (or use any other label, for that matter). We can now see ourselves as normal people; the anxiety or agoraphobia becomes an inconsequential part of our total self-image.

Recovery does not mean we'll never feel anxious again; no one can expect to be completely anxiety-free. But the anxiety will diminish and become much more manageable. The more we lower our expectations for a perfect recovery, the stronger a recovery we can actually bring about. The more time we give ourselves, the sooner we will recover. Such paradoxes are difficult to accept and understand. At first, they seem neither logical nor helpful. As you read this book, however, the many paradoxes of the recovery process will become more understandable. This understanding will make the recovery process easier.

Recovery means more than being free of panic or anxiety; it also means personal growth and awareness. In recovery, we look back and realize that we have made it through a very difficult time. This realization leaves us with a feeling of great accomplishment. We gain valuable insights and learn coping skills that can change our lives.

PART 2

THE SOLUTION: A COGNITIVE APPROACH

It amazes me how far I have come on my road to recovery. . . . I would have never believed life could be so sweet.

—DEBBY

INTRODUCTION TO THE PROGRAM

Embracing the Fear offers a three-part program: (A) Managing Our Anxiety, (B) Listening to Our Inner Dialogue, and (C) Lifestyle Awareness. "Managing Our Anxiety" offers strategies for dealing with panic attacks, as well as chronic or generalized anxiety. "Listening to Our Inner Dialogue" explains how our self-talk plays an important part in initiating and perpetuating our anxiety and panic, as well as helping us make it more manageable. Specific examples are included. "Lifestyle Awareness" helps us gain a better understanding of how we feel about ourselves and how we relate to others. It raises our awareness of how we deal with everyday life events and how our way of dealing with them can set us up for anxiety or panic reactions.

These three components appear together in sequence in this part of the book for each of fourteen separate issues. This format allows us to focus on one issue at a time and to see a correlation between how we deal with our anxiety or panic and how we deal with everyday life events. Each anxiety management strategy and related inner dialogue ties in with an interior Lifestyle Awareness dialogue and a testimonial.

If the program could be condensed into one word, it would be *allow*. Throughout the book we are encouraged to allow our thoughts, feelings, anxiety—and even panic. We are encouraged to accept them and at times even invite them. Nowhere in the program are we told that we must do something about our anxiety (such as getting rid of it or controlling it). We try not to use words like *should, must,* and *have to*, because they belong to a coping style that promotes unmanageable anxiety. Instead, we encourage a more adaptive style of coping, one that is more permissive of failure and puts less emphasis on obligation and the need to perform perfectly.

Because this book addresses several audiences, we refer interchangeably to agoraphobia, phobia, panic, panic disorder, anxiety, and anxiety disorders.

A: *Managing Our Anxiety*

"Managing Our Anxiety" differs from other anxiety management programs in that it encourages a comprehensive permissive approach in dealing with anxiety. It allows us to experience the process of recovery without putting demands on us. In other words, it gives us permission to have the problem. It does not give us the message that we *have to* relax or that we *must* stop thinking catastrophic thoughts. It does not tell us that we must *force* ourselves to generate positive affirmations that are both unbelievable and impossible to internalize. Nor does it insist we *compel* ourselves to *never* withdraw from an unmanageable situation. These demands fit into the kind of self-talk that has already contributed to our problems with anxiety. To many, the ideas in this book may seem paradoxical and irrational, but they involve a most natural and effective approach to recovery.

Relaxation. One of the most important ideas in this program is that we needn't be insistent on relaxation. This is not to say that relaxation isn't helpful. Naturally, a comfortable state of relaxation is desirable, especially since a panic attack seems inconsistent with relaxation. However, for those of us with an anxiety disorder, telling ourselves that we *have to* get hold of ourselves or that we *have to* relax only adds more pressure to our anxiety state. When we find relaxation difficult, we feel we have failed at a task anyone should be able to accomplish. What we need to do, in fact, is to *learn how to be anxious*. The first step in learning how to relax is letting go of the need to relax and allowing the anxiety to be there. In other words, we first need to give ourselves permission to have the problem. Then we can begin to do something about it.

The escape/avoidance problem. This program takes a complex position with regard to the escape/avoidance problem. It is true that we often escape from situations in which we are anxious or in which we experience a panic attack. It is also true that following this experience, we often avoid that same situation. Eventually, similar situations—often less threatening than the original—now cause fear. As we continue to avoid, our world becomes smaller, resulting occasionally in unwillingness to venture outside the safety of home. A typical situation is that of the agoraphobic who experiences a panic attack at a large mall and escapes the mall, vowing never to return again. Soon he or she avoids all large malls, then avoids smaller shopping centers, since anxiety or panic attacks could occur there also. Finally, over a period of time, even the neighborhood grocery store is avoided.

It might appear that all we would need to do is refrain from escaping and avoiding feared situations. Unfortunately the answer is not that simple. We usually try very hard *not* to escape from feared situations, and if we do, we try equally hard not to avoid them later on. The instructions we give ourselves are complex: on the one hand, we tell ourselves we cannot stay and therefore we have to leave; but on the other hand, we tell ourselves we cannot leave—that would be shameful and cowardly—and so we have to stay.

It is impossible to stay in a place and leave it at the same time. And yet this is exactly what we are forcing ourselves to do. Since all the possible options are ruled out, we are left with no choices. This is a classic double-bind situation. The result is that we feel trapped, unable to stay and unable to leave. And when we feel trapped we are likely to experience panic. This is the most plausible reason panic attacks are so likely to occur in feared situations. This is also why escape and avoidance behaviors are so persistent and cannot be stopped by simply telling ourselves to do so.

The solution lies in seeing that *both* remaining in *and* leaving the feared situation are equally acceptable. It is not enough to encourage ourselves to stay in a feared situation, for that deals with only half the problem. It is equally important for us to realize that we truly are able and free to leave a feared situation any time we wish. Once we grant ourselves permission to leave, staying gradually becomes easier, for a major obstacle will have been removed.

Catastrophic thoughts. There is a certain kind of fear, often called a fear of fear, that has a catastrophic quality about it. It is usually signaled by the phrase "What if?" For example: *What if I go to the shopping mall and I faint?* Or, *What if I drive on the freeway, have a panic attack, lose control, and cause an accident!* Such thoughts are alarming, and there are many who believe we should learn to control such thoughts.

Such thoughts are harmless in themselves, even if they cause alarm or discomfort. In fact, that is exactly what they should do. It is not a bad idea to have a catastrophic thought about getting into an accident on the freeway; such thoughts could alert us to the need to be extra careful while driving. But what is troublesome about catastrophic thoughts is that they occur with such frequency. They also seem to have a life of their own. The more we try to control them or eliminate them, such as by distracting ourselves from them, the more troublesome they seem to become. Perhaps they are so frequent and so automatic because we try so hard not to have them and not to be alarmed by them.

When we have catastrophic thoughts, much more than mere thought is taking place. Our minds become very busy at this point and start to apply deep interpretations to these thoughts and devise strategies for dealing with them. One example of a deep interpretation is the idea that such thoughts are abnormal or defective: *Why am I having such thoughts? They are ridiculous! I shouldn't think this way!* There is no compelling reason why any of us should think this way, but the fact is that we do think this way about our catastrophic thoughts. If we were to examine the self-talk in this paragraph, we would notice that it has a common theme: *shame.*

Here are the program's fourteen anxiety management strategies.

1. We will try to accept the fact that we sometimes feel out of control of our lives because of feelings of anxiety or panic. By accepting the fact that we have an anxiety disorder, without passing judgment on ourselves, we have taken a major step in recovery.

2. Our self-talk, which tends to be shaming and nonpermissive, has been partly responsible for our anxiety or panic. It continues to be a problem because it affects the intensity and duration of these feelings. It will help if we practice an inner dialogue that is nurturing. We might begin by giving ourselves permission to be anxious.

3. We will try to allow the sensations of anxiety or panic, not resisting them but just letting them happen. It will help if we do not attach danger to these feelings.

4. When feeling anxious, we will try to slow down, not only in our actions but in our thinking as well. When we feel a need to rush ahead, it will help if we try to focus on the moment.

5. With the onset of intense anxiety or panic, our first reaction is to try to stay in control. It will help if we practice letting go; the less we attempt to stay in control, the more in control we will feel.

6. We will try to take risks rather than continually avoid places and situations where we feel anxious. It will help if we reassure ourselves that we are not in any danger and that we *can* function well even when we're uncomfortable.

7. When catastrophizing with the what-ifs, we will try to be permissive of them and not fight them. It will help to realize that they are only thoughts and that chances are they will not happen. It might also help to affirm that we carry our safety within.

8. We will try to develop a more helpful attitude toward our anxiety disorder by learning more about it, thus removing the veil of mystery. By talking about it, we also lift the burden of a deep, dark secret.

9. When approaching a situation where we feel anxious, we will try to take it one step at a time, keeping our expectations low. It will help if we think of it as an opportunity to *practice*.

10. We will try to accept setbacks as a normal and necessary part of our recovery, trying to see them as temporary. It might help to remind ourselves that even though we feel as if we're starting over, we never really go back to square one.

11. We will try to take the time limit out of our recovery, seeing it as open-ended. It will help if we try to accept where we are right now without comparing ourselves with past progress, and at the same time, try to be accepting of the possibility of any future anxiety.

12. During our process of recovery, we can reach a point where we no longer anticipate the occurrence of panic attacks. When we no longer care whether we panic, the attacks will eventually subside.

13. Although we sometimes feel helpless, we might try to be receptive to the idea that each of us has inner strength to draw upon when necessary.

14. As we gain a better understanding of our anxiety problem and move ahead in our recovery, we can continue to benefit by reaching out to others who need support and encouragement.

B: Listening to Our Inner Dialogue

Inner dialogue is a vital part of this program, since our self-talk has played an important part in precipitating and maintaining our anxiety problem. What we say to ourselves at the onset of a panic attack can affect its severity and duration. It can also affect our perception of the problem itself. For instance, if we see our anxiety or panic as shameful or unacceptable, we will tap into a self-shaming and non-permissive inner dialogue, or "A-talk." For example, *This is terrible! I shouldn't have this problem! There must be something terribly wrong with me!* All of these thoughts are alarming and only serve to add anxiety to an already anxious state.

The essence of A-talk is an abusive and dehumanizing system of managing our life. It is intolerant of imperfection and failure and insistent on perfection and approval. It is this system that constantly creates problems for us.

Recovery depends on being able to set up a different way of managing our feelings, thoughts, and behaviors. This new system, labeled "B-talk," needs to compete with the old system (A-talk). B-talk cannot replace the old system, because it is impossible to get rid of. In fact, the more we try to do that, the more troublesome the A-talk becomes. The biggest problem with the A-talk is that it has become highly ingrained in our personality. Therefore, it is likely to persist and to be automatic for some time to come. The best we can do at first is to try to generate the new system as a competing way of interpreting and dealing with problems in general, and with our anxiety disorder in particular.

The new system offers ideas to counter those of the old system. It processes information about ourselves and the world around us in a fundamentally different way; it is a self-nurturing and nonshaming way of interpreting events. It is highly tolerant of the self and permissive of imperfection and failure. B-talk does not insist on perfection, or try to get rid of or control anything. Rather, it tries to be allowing of scary feelings, catastrophic thoughts, avoidance behavior, and even relapses. It is a highly humanizing voice that accepts us as we are, including our perceived imperfections and our catastrophic thoughts.

One of our first tasks is to become as familiar as possible with our A-talk. As we do, the connection between our A-talk and our distress becomes increasingly clear. At some point the question arises as to what to do about the A-talk: Do we control it? Do we get rid of it? If we were to follow such an approach, we would be dealing with our A-talk through more A-talk. A more effective approach is to incorporate a more nurturing inner dialogue (B-talk) to directly compete with the A-talk, so that there is some balance between the two.

At first this new system will be almost impossible to get going, and the old system will keep on operating and keep on making us miserable. But this is to be expected. Slowly and gradually, however, the B-talk will become internalized; it will become the natural way of coping with events. When this happens, we will have reached an important point in the recovery process.

C: Lifestyle Awareness

As mentioned earlier, each anxiety management strategy and its related inner dialogue corresponds to a lifestyle awareness topic, which allows us to see a correlation between how we deal with our anxiety or panic and how we deal with everyday life events.

The lifestyle awareness discussion does not give advice, nor does it tell us how to make changes in our lives. Its purpose is to raise our level of awareness of how we deal with everyday life situations and how this affects our anxiety level. In most cases it simply reframes the situation so we can see it from a more helpful perspective. In some cases it suggests an alternative approach.

Whereas the anxiety management strategies help us manage our symptoms, the lifestyle awareness topics make us aware of possible environmental sources of anxiety and panic. The goal is to gain a better understanding of how we feel about ourselves and how we relate to others. We often discover that we are stuck in some area of our life, whether it's our lifestyle, career, relationship, or belief system. As we grow in this awareness, we begin to see that there is a relationship between our feeling of helplessness and our anxiety. We come to realize that we have options that can help us make the desired changes in our lives. During our recovery we become more and more aware that panic attacks do not come from out of the blue—they are there for a reason.

Here are the fourteen topics of Lifestyle Awareness:

1. We are aware that we can be our own worst critic. It will help if we can try to be less self-critical by being more gentle with ourselves, accepting our limitations as well as our strengths.

2. We are aware that it will help to practice a nurturing inner dialogue, one that is more permissive and accepting of ourselves. We might begin by being aware of the "shoulds" in our self-talk.

3. We are aware of the importance of being in touch with and expressing our feelings. It will help if we try to allow ourselves to experience and express them without judgment or denial.

4. We are aware that we have a tendency to take life at a fast pace. It will help if we try to slow down, make fewer demands on ourselves, and take time to experience the present.

5. We are aware that we sometimes feel out of control of our lives, which can leave us feeling trapped and helpless. We will try to let go, allow for more spontaneity, and see ourselves as having options.

6. We are aware that we often choose avoidance as a way of dealing with difficult situations. It would be more helpful to try to work through these difficulties. If we cannot bring about a change, it will help if we try to generate a new perception of the situation so that we will not feel trapped or helpless.

7. We are aware that our tendency to catastrophize makes it difficult to be receptive to positive outcomes. It will help if we are permissive of our thoughts, both positive and negative, rather than feeling that we have to block them out or replace them with other thoughts.

8. We are aware that we sometimes avoid processing difficult events in our lives by not thinking about them or by distorting their meaning. It will help if we take a good look at them and try to see the meaning they have for us.

9. We are aware of our need for perfectionism. It will help if we allow ourselves to be average rather than to continually strive

for perfection. We might remind ourselves that making mistakes does not have to affect our self-worth.

10. We are aware that we have a difficult time dealing with failure, seeing it as further evidence of low self-worth. It will help if we give ourselves the freedom to fail, considering it an opportunity for growth.

11. We are aware that it helps to live one day at a time, while slowly coming to terms with the past and letting the future take care of itself.

12. We are aware that we have difficulty being flexible and that we tend to see things in all-or-nothing terms. It will help if we try to be less absolute in our thinking, allowing more flexibility in our lives.

13. We are aware that many of us are dealing with low self-esteem. We will try to be more accepting of good feelings about ourselves.

14. We are aware that we feel better when we are actively involved, whether we are working, helping others, or pursuing leisure-time activities.

STRATEGY 1

A. MANAGING OUR ANXIETY: ACCEPTING OUR ANXIETY DISORDER

We will try to accept the fact that we sometimes feel out of control of our lives because of feelings of anxiety or panic. By accepting the fact that we have an anxiety disorder, without passing judgment on ourselves, we have taken a major step in recovery.

Acceptance begins with admitting that we have an anxiety disorder, one that in some cases has precipitated a vicious circle of panic and avoidance. Acceptance means facing the fact that there is no immediate cure, no miracle drug at hand. It means realizing that our symptoms will most likely persist for some time; they will not go away just because we want them to. Denying that we have a problem, trying not to think about it, or telling ourselves how unacceptable it is tends only to frighten and confuse us more and increase the feeling of being trapped.

As we move through this maze of fear and confusion, we are consumed with a sense of impending doom, convinced that there is something terribly wrong with us. Because of the nature of our symptoms, we can spend a great deal of time and energy on doctors and medical tests, trying to find a physical cause for our problem, only to be told that we are in good health and that perhaps our problem is emotional. When it is suggested that we seek professional psychological help, we become even more alarmed. We feel that having an emotional problem or seeing a therapist is shaming and stigmatizing. Somewhere along the way we have been given the message that we should be in control of our emotions.

For several reasons, we hang on to the belief that we are dealing with a physical problem. The intensity of symptoms convinces us that this has to be more serious than a case of nerves. We also believe that a physical illness is so much easier to fix: psychotherapy could take years just to get to the cause of the problem. Finally, seeing the symptoms as physical rather than emotional tends to alleviate our feeling of shame. Unfortunately, focusing exclusively on the physical can slow down the recovery process.

Trying to get a new perspective on the situation and adopting a more permissive inner dialogue can be very helpful. Giving ourselves permission to have this problem is the first step in accepting our anxiety. It might help if we remind ourselves that no one is entirely free of problems. Some people have tension headaches or a chronic illness; we get a rush of adrenaline at unexpected times. So be it! The more we can see our problem as normal for our situation and the more we can accept it, the better. Those who are diagnosed early are fortunate. However, just because some of us have suffered with an anxiety disorder longer does not necessarily mean that it will take years of therapy to recover.

Once we know what we are dealing with, it is advisable to find a therapist who specializes in treating anxiety disorders. A support group that is well-facilitated and based on a structured program is also helpful. When we are in contact with others who face the same problem, we no longer feel so isolated and alone.

Learning about our anxiety disorder is essential, as it is difficult to be accepting when we do not know what is happening to us. It might take some time before we truly accept that we have this problem. Merely telling ourselves that we do accept it will not necessarily make our symptoms go away, at least not at first. Sometimes we will be able to accept, and other times we won't. In the beginning, the best we can do is to try to live with the discomfort. However long it might take, accepting the fact that we have an anxiety disorder and still feeling okay about ourselves constitute a major step in our recovery.

B. Listening to Our Inner Dialogue:
Nonacceptance/Acceptance

We tell ourselves that having this problem is unacceptable. It is shameful and therefore not permissible. Defects of character are not to be tolerated. If we allow such defects to be there, they will only get worse. Since nonpermissive self-talk is highly internalized, acceptance will not come easily. We can, however, try to be more accepting of what is happening to us; we can adopt a more nurturing inner dialogue to balance the A-talk and B-talk.

A-Talk: Nonacceptance	*B-Talk: Acceptance*
1. This is ridiculous, stupid, crazy! I shouldn't have this problem.	1. Even though this might seem stupid or crazy, it's not. This is all a part of having an anxiety disorder.
2. What's wrong with me? This isn't normal!	2. I have a panic disorder. The feelings I'm having are normal for what I'm dealing with. It will help if I can be accepting of that.
3. Why am I feeling this way? I'm an adult and I shouldn't have these fears.	3. These feelings are part of having an anxiety problem, and it's okay to have them. Shaming myself will only make matters worse.
4. My friends and family will think I'm crazy.	4. This problem is difficult for other people to understand. I'll try to feel okay about myself regardless of what others might think.
5. I don't see anyone else dealing with something like this. Why me?	5. Everyone deals with something. For me it is a chronic fear of intense anxiety or panic attacks. So be it!
6. I'm so embarrassed about this. What if someone finds out?	6. It's okay to be phobic. I don't have to be embarrassed about it. The more I can give myself permission to be this way, the less of a problem it will be.

C. LIFESTYLE AWARENESS: ACCEPTING OUR LIMITATIONS

We are aware that we can be our own worst critic. It will help if we can try to be less self-critical by being more gentle with ourselves, accepting our limitations as well as our strengths.

Raising Our Level of Awareness

1. We tend to allow other people to make mistakes, but we are quick to judge our own actions.

1. We might try to be more gentle with ourselves, by being less self-critical and giving ourselves more freedom to make mistakes. We might remind ourselves that our mistakes will not affect our self-worth.

2. We often focus on our limitations, feeling that what we do just isn't good enough.

2. We will try to recognize our strengths, even though we know this will be difficult. It will also help if we can be more accepting of our limitations.

3. We sometimes feel inferior and compare ourselves unfavorably with others.

3. Rather than putting ourselves down, we could try to accept and appreciate ourselves and our good qualities.

4. We worry about how we're viewed by others. (Criticism confirms any negative feelings we might have about ourselves.)

4. It will help if we remind ourselves that our concern isn't so much about what other people might think about us, but how we feel about what people might think about us, and how we feel about ourselves.

Although recovery is due to a combination of many different factors, acceptance plays a large part in the process. Lynn explains how accepting where she is in her recovery has made a difference.

> *At a recent support group meeting, a young man asked, "Does anyone else get up in the morning dreading a panic attack?" Now, I can remember feeling that way, but to my surprise I realized I no longer think about that. This question made me reflect on how far I've come. I know that I might have setbacks, but I also know that "allowing" them to happen, getting lots of practice, and accepting where I am now in my recovery help me through the tough moments. I used to panic everywhere—church, movie theaters,*

restaurants, home, social functions. I thought I was nuts! I avoided most of these places in fear of the dreaded attack. However, I am enjoying my successes now and it's wonderful!

I took the risk and enrolled in a floral class, which I've wanted to do for a long time. I was not comfortable the first couple of times, but I told myself, That's okay, I'm bound to be anxious, and besides, maybe there are others here feeling the same way. From then on it was great; I hated to see the first session end. I am now enrolled in two more sessions and can't wait to begin again.

STRATEGY 2

A. MANAGING OUR ANXIETY: PRACTICING A SELF-NURTURING INNER DIALOGUE

Our self-talk, which tends to be shaming and nonpermissive, has been partly responsible for our anxiety or panic. It continues to be a problem because it affects the intensity and duration of these feelings. It will help if we practice an inner dialogue that is nurturing. We might begin by giving ourselves permission to be anxious.

Underlying our anxiety is an inner dialogue that is intolerant and critical of ourselves. Seeing our anxiety or panic as unacceptable, we belittle ourselves. We accuse ourselves of being irrational and tell ourselves that we have to do something about our problem. Our inner dialogue says, *Figure out what makes you anxious and get rid of it or change it.* The same holds true for our catastrophic thoughts, our avoidance behavior, and our setbacks. This nonpermissive and shaming A-talk is a self-degrading approach to dealing with this and other problems. It would help to be more aware of our A-talk and to try to incorporate a more nurturing inner dialogue, B-talk. B-talk is a highly permissive coping style; it allows us to have intense anxiety and panic attacks, to have catastrophic thoughts, and to go through setbacks. It allows us to have feelings of discouragement, disappointment, and depression. B-talk does not come naturally to us, since our inner dialogue is permeated with A-talk. A-talk is largely responsible for our difficulties with anxiety and panic. Once we realize this, we might think that the answer is quite simple—all we have to do is replace the A-talk with B-talk. However, since A-talk is so internalized— imprinted in our personality, so to speak—it is not easy to rid ourselves of it. What we can do at first is listen to our A-talk and appreciate the extent to which it creates problems for us. Then we can try to generate some B-talk, with the hope of establishing a dialogue between our A-talk and our B-talk, between our nonpermissive and our permissive thoughts.

What we say to ourselves when we are feeling anxious or at the onset of panic can make a difference in how we handle the feared situation. No matter how many times we have had these feelings, our first reaction has been to ask ourselves, *What's happening to me?* We then come up with any number of frightening answers. The question itself signals danger, and our inner dialogue continues to frighten us as we react to the mounting panic. Our response is to become alarmed by the fearful thoughts. This precipitates more alarm, which sets off a complex cycle of A-talk and escalating catastrophic thoughts until we feel out of control.

We use this kind of self-talk because we don't understand what is happening to us. After all, we have good reason to be alarmed when feelings of such intensity seem to come out of nowhere. What would help is to try to make sense of what is happening in a simple and accurate way, e.g., *I'm anxious because of the stressful events that are going on in my life*, or, *I'm anxious because I have an anxiety problem*. Making sense of our anxiety is not the same as being extremely rational or analytical or intellectual. It is a simple, nonshaming way of dealing with this problem. We want to understand why we're anxious. We then want to look at it and tell ourselves that it's all right to have these feelings. If we can approach the task of understanding our problem in ways that are simple and more or less accurate, we will be on our way toward demystifying the problem. As we improve our understanding and awareness of how anxiety and phobias work, we are also better able to come up with a more nurturing way of talking to ourselves. Adopting an inner dialogue that is supportive and non-shaming helps us in our recovery.

B. LISTENING TO OUR INNER DIALOGUE: NONPERMISSIVE/PERMISSIVE

Being unaccepting and intolerant of our unwanted thoughts, feelings, and behaviors seems like a logical and helpful strategy: the less tolerant we are, the more motivated we will be to eliminate them. Unfortunately, it is not that easy. Such a strategy is not only ineffective but also often leads to reinforcement of the unwanted thoughts, feelings, and behaviors. On the one hand, doing battle with them aggravates them and intensifies our fears; on the other hand, simply allowing them to run their course dilutes their importance. We can start by being more permissive of our anxiety and by encouraging ourselves to become more tolerant of whatever we experience—especially, of ourselves and our perceived deficiencies.

A-Talk: Nonpermissive	*B-Talk: Permissive*
1. What's wrong with me? Why am I so anxious?	1. I'm probably anxious because. . . (Offer a simple explanation, e.g., I didn't sleep well last night, my job is very stressful these days, I need to slow down.)
2. This shouldn't be happening to me! I must be dying (or passing out, going crazy, etc.)!	2. I'm having a panic attack. It's only the thought of dying that is frightening me. It's all right to have frightening thoughts. I'm not in any physical danger.
3. I can't go on like this! I just have to get hold of myself!	3. Chances are this feeling isn't going to go away just because I want it to. I'll try to be open to the thought that I just might be uncomfortable for a while.
4. This is ridiculous! It's all in my head. I've got to pull myself together!	4. I'm really being hard on myself. I don't have to do anything other than just let the fearful thoughts (anxiety) happen. Sometimes the best I can do is to muddle through and then try to be okay with that.
5. This is terrible! Nothing seems to be working. I just can't stand this anymore!	5. This is very difficult, but I may be trying too hard. It will help if I allow these feelings to just be there and perhaps remind myself that "this too shall pass."

C. LIFESTYLE AWARENESS: BEING LESS SELF-CRITICAL

We are aware that it will help to practice a nurturing inner dialogue, one that is more permissive and accepting of ourselves. We might begin by being aware of the "shoulds" in our self-talk.

Raising Our Level of Awareness

1. Our self-talk has played a major role in our anxiety problem. We continue to use nonpermissive strategies. For example, we tell ourselves we shouldn't have certain feelings, that it's not okay to express our needs or make certain decisions in our lives.

1. It will help if we try to adopt a more nurturing inner dialogue, one that is permissive and accepting of ourselves rather than critical and judgmental.

2. Our self-talk is permeated with "shoulds" that do not allow any options.

2. We might try to think in terms of "It would be nice if . . ." or "I would like to . . ."

3. We sometimes verbally abuse ourselves with such adjectives as *silly, ridiculous,* and *irrational.*

3. We might start trying to recognize and appreciate our fine qualities, being more receptive to an accepting and supportive inner dialogue. But even more important, we can try to accept any perceived deficiencies or inadequacies. The more accepting we are of these, the better we will feel about ourselves.

4. We often feel inadequate and have a hard time allowing ourselves to have good feelings about ourselves, making it difficult to foster a self-nurturing inner dialogue.

4. As our self-esteem improves and we progressively feel better about ourselves, the big challenge will be to allow ourselves to be permissive of these good feelings and adopt a more nurturing inner dialogue.

The more we can give ourselves permission to be uncomfortable, the better. So often we test ourselves by seeing how well we can do in feared situations. Our self-talk tends to say, *Let's see if I can do this without feeling anxious.* It would be more helpful to say, *I will most likely be anxious, since this is where I usually have difficulty. I'll try to see this as an opportunity to practice allowing any anxiety I might experience.*

In the following testimonial, Sharon explains how her inner dialogue helped her with driving.

> *I would just like to share a few good things, hoping to encourage those who feel that this is never going to get better. It will! Driving has been difficult for me, but last summer I made two trips. One was a four- to five-hour drive to my mom's, where I spent a week fishing with my son. It was great! By keeping my expectations low and giving myself permission to turn back at any time, I managed to get there with little or no problem. But I felt quite uncomfortable coming home. This is where a self-nurturing inner dialogue was very helpful. I gave myself permission to pull over, stop, rest if necessary, and then continue on. It worked! I made it home absolutely thrilled with what I'd done.*
>
> *Next I went on an overnight retreat in a town several hours from home. I drove with a friend. Again I kept my expectations low, allowing for any discomfort. As it turned out, we had a great time! I was able to do things I hadn't done in a long time. I look back on this experience as a real victory.*

STRATEGY 3

A. Managing Our Anxiety: Allowing the Sensations of Anxiety or Panic

We will try to allow the sensations of anxiety or panic, not resisting them but just letting them happen. It will help if we do not attach danger to these feelings.

There is nothing easy about "allowing" or "going with" the feeling when dealing with unmanageable anxiety or riding the wave of a panic attack. As our anxiety builds in intensity, we find ourselves fighting it every step of the way. We feel that the more we tense up and hang on, the more successful we will be in warding off the uncontrollable feelings. Unfortunately, the more we resist them, the more anxious we become, and we find ourselves helplessly caught up in a vicious circle of fear and panic. All thoughts of allowing or going with the feeling are quickly abandoned. With each strange sensation, we're quick to analyze what we *think* might be happening to us, and the more we focus on these thoughts, the more frightened we become. We feel that we are truly in some kind of danger—a perfectly valid feeling. However, an awareness of what is really happening will be helpful at this point. What we are dealing with is the *thought* of what we're afraid might happen, not the actual event. And it is the *thought* that is causing us to panic or to experience intense anxiety. By telling ourselves this—reassuring ourselves that it is only a feeling and that we are not in any physical danger—we can recognize the panic for what it is and then give ourselves permission to experience it.

The key to this strategy is the phrase "There is no danger!" Once we are at least somewhat sure of this fact (we're never really completely convinced), we're in a better position to work with the feelings themselves. After all, if we really think that we're going to make a fool of ourselves, we will be somewhat reluctant to just let it happen. Or if a feeling of impending doom convinces us that we're in some kind of danger, we're going to have a difficult time focusing on words such as *accept* and *allow*. Feelings of panic or intense anxiety are difficult enough to deal with when we recognize them for what they are. So until we can reassure ourselves that we are not in any danger, we're in for a rough ride.

When we stop focusing on the physical symptoms and realize it is only a thought that triggers the anxiety or panic, we find it's a little easier to accept, allow, and go with the feeling. Sometimes this means doing nothing at all, because no matter what we try, it just doesn't seem to help. It is important to be okay with that—in other words, to give ourselves permission to muddle through the best we can and to allow the frustration that goes with muddling. Fretting over the fact that nothing seems to be working, and then fretting over the fact that we are frustrated because nothing seems to be working, only adds to our stress.

We could try to see the next onset of anxiety or panic as a reaction to a thought and reassure ourselves that we are not in any physical danger. It will help if we give ourselves permission to have the symptoms without overanalyzing them or trying to distract ourselves. We can also rely on helpful coping strategies, whether that means allowing and going with the feeling or just muddling through!

B. LISTENING TO OUR INNER DIALOGUE: NONPERMISSIVE/PERMISSIVE

We tell ourselves that certain feelings are shameful or unacceptable and must be done away with. Otherwise, they'll just go on forever. The idea is that the more strenuously we try, the more efficiently we'll get rid of things. As logical as that might sound, it doesn't work that way in this particular situation. The paradox is, the less effort we put forth, the more efficient we'll become in achieving our goal.

A-Talk: Nonpermissive	*B-Talk Permissive*
1. I have to stop being so anxious! I must relax!	1. I'll try to allow the anxiety to be there. I do not have to force myself to relax.
2. If I don't do something about this anxiety, it's really going to get out of hand.	2. It's better if I let go and allow the anxiety to do what it wants, without my trying to stop it.

A-Talk: *Nonpermissive*	B-Talk *Permissive*
3. I feel like I'm going pieces. I've got to get hold of myself!	3. I'm not really going to pieces. I only feel that way. It will help if I can allow that feeling.
4. There must be something terribly wrong with me. This just isn't normal.	4. There's nothing wrong with me other than the fact that I'm feeling anxious (or sensitized).
5. I'm letting this get the best of me. Maybe if I just don't think about it, it will go away.	5. Trying hard not to think about it doesn't always work. It's better if I can just stay with the feeling and try not to fight it.

C. Lifestyle Awareness: Being in Touch with and Expressing Our Feelings

We are aware of the importance of being in touch with and expressing our feelings. It will help if we try to allow ourselves to experience and express them without judgment or denial.

Raising Our Level of Awareness

1. Many of us learned to repress our feelings when we were very young, usually because of criticism we received for expressing them. Repressed feelings contribute to our anxiety problem.	1. It will help if we see our feelings as normal, necessary experiences and allow ourselves to express them. When this is difficult to do, we might consider keeping a journal to record them.
2. We don't always see our feelings as being valid or important, giving our-selves the message, *It's not okay to feel this way.* However, denying our feelings can leave us open to anxiety or panic.	2. It will be easier to be in touch with our feelings, and allow them to be there, if we try to see them as valid.

3. Our perfectionism keeps our feelings under control. Expressing our emotions (anger, sadness, fear) feels like losing control. We are afraid this could result in criticism, alienation, or abandonment.

3. It will help if we practice expressing our feelings even at the risk of being criticized, alienated, or abandoned.

4. As with other feelings we would rather not deal with, we tend to push feelings of guilt aside.

4. We might try to deal with guilt as we would any other emotion. Once we have faced it and worked through it, it will be easier to let go of it.

In the following testimonial, Anne talks about having several panic attacks while driving to the art museum. Her story demonstrates the effectiveness of staying with the feelings and allowing ourselves to experience anxiety or panic attacks.

> *While visiting the art museum, I walked past a Grant Wood painting and was reminded of the time my daughter wanted to see the Grant Wood exhibit when it was in town. Far be it from me to ever deny my children such an experience; however, we lived in the suburbs, and I was agoraphobic. The art museum seemed to be at the other end of the earth. The mere thought of driving there was overwhelming. Needless to say, we never made it.*
>
> *Later, when I was in therapy, the museum was one of the places my therapist took me for a practice session. It was like a reawakening to life. During my recovery, I returned there many times on my own. On one such occasion I experienced several panic attacks while driving to the museum. I gave myself permission to turn back, but each time I continued on, using the attacks as an opportunity to practice some of the strategies that I was learning in therapy. First, I acknowledged the fact that they were only panic attacks, that they were only feelings, and that I was in no danger. Rather than fighting the feelings, I tried to stay with them and focused on moving in slow motion. It worked! Before I knew it, I was over halfway there. And the rest of the way was smooth sailing.*

Once I was there, I continued to deal with a whole new set of symptoms. Again I reassured myself that these were only feelings and that it would help to stay with them rather than block them out. I told myself that I could leave at any time, which was important, since it kept me from feeling trapped. It was that thought that actually helped me to stay. When I finally did leave, I did so in tears. It wasn't because I felt I'd failed, but because I was painfully aware of all that I had been missing. I was still asking questions like Why me? Why can't I stay here and enjoy myself like everyone else? What's wrong with me? Am I ever going to get well? As time went on, my inner dialogue sounded more like Well, this is who I am today. It just might be this way for a while. It's okay to feel this way. And, This too shall pass.

Considering the many hours I've spent at the art museum since those early days, whether visiting or working as a volunteer, it's difficult to believe that there was ever a time when I avoided going there.

❧

A. MANAGING OUR ANXIETY: SLOWING DOWN

When feeling anxious, we will try to slow down, not only in our actions but in our thinking as well. When we feel a need to rush ahead, it will help if we try to focus on the moment.

At the onset of anxiety or panic, our automatic reaction is to speed up to put an end to our discomfort as soon as possible. The more we hurry, however, the more anxious we become. It's helpful to identify this need to speed up and to recognize that it's subconscious. Once we acknowledge and understand this need, we are in a position to try a different approach—slowing down.

Even when we slow down, our thoughts still tend to rush. Whether we are on the expressway or in the mall, with the first wave of anxiety or panic our mind rushes ahead to the nearest exit—signaling the need to escape—and we are caught up in a vicious circle of intense anxiety or panic. What helps is to try to slow *everything* down and focus on the moment, allowing each wave of anxiety to run its course. Even if we choose to leave an uncomfortable situation, it helps to escape *slowly*. Doing so can help us keep alert to what we are doing, as well as remind us to use the helpful B-talk and to stay calm. Finally, reminding ourselves to slow down will be more effective if we see it as an option and not as a must: *If I have a difficult time slowing down, so be it. But I'll try the best I can.*

Other helpful strategies include the following:

- Visualizing ourselves moving in slow motion
- Actually moving or walking in slow motion
- Visualizing ourselves moving into a panic attack rather than away from it; in effect, mentally embracing the fear

We might try to visualize ourselves slowing down in a feared situation *before* the actual event. This would give us some practice in dealing with the anxiety and help us cope better at the time. With some practice, and if we so choose, diaphragmatic breathing can keep us from hyperventilating. (See Appendix for the section "Some Thoughts on Self-Care.") Remember, we do not have to do anything to "fix" it, but we do have the option to choose certain strategies that might be helpful.

Recovery can be a slow process and our A-talk tells us to seek quick solutions. As frustrating as it may be, coming to terms with the idea that recovery takes time may be helpful. The more we slow down, the less troublesome our anxiety will be; the less hurried we are to get over our anxiety problem, the more quickly we can recover from it. If we allow ourselves to experience the process without trying to rush through it, we can actually be strengthened by it. Rushing through the recovery process is self-defeating because it denies us the opportunity to learn and grow.

B. Listening to Our Inner Dialogue: Accelerating/Slowing Down

We tend to see speed as desirable. We believe it guarantees that we will get things done quickly and more efficiently, so the faster we get things done, the better off we will be. Our inner dialogue says, *I can't let time pass, because if I do, it will pass me by.* We feel that escape from an anxious situation needs to be done as quickly as possible.

A-Talk: Accelerating	*B-Talk: Slowing Down*
1. I hate this! I wish this anxiety would go away now! I've got to find a solution quickly!	1. Wishing the anxiety away doesn't help. I'll try to slow down and allow it to be there.
2. I've got to get out of here! I can't take this anymore! Leaving is the fastest way to put an end to this.	2. It's okay to leave, but it helps to escape slowly.
3. I'd better hurry up before the anxiety gets worse and I have a full-blown panic attack!	3. It's better if I just take my time. Hurrying is a sure way to bring on feelings of panic.
4. If this doesn't go away soon, it will continue to get worse, and who knows what might happen to me!	4. The more I try to speed up my recovery, the more anxious I feel. It's possible that my anxiety might get worse for a while. I'll try to be okay with that.

A-Talk: Accelerating

5. Why doesn't this go away? It seems like it's going to last forever! I've got to get rid of this problem right now!

B-Talk: Slowing Down

5. The less I hurry to get over this, the more quickly I'll recover.

C. LIFESTYLE AWARENESS: SLOWING DOWN

We are aware that we have a tendency to take life at a fast pace. It will help if we try to slow down, make fewer demands on ourselves, and take time to experience the present.

Raising Our Level of Awareness

1. One of the worst problems we face is speeding up, because it constantly stirs up our anxiety.

1. We will try to be aware of our pace and practice slowing down as much as possible, even when those around us are rushing.

2. Perfectionism coerces the mind to take on more than it can handle, which only adds to the need to rush.

2. It will help if we give ourselves permission to take on less each day and then prioritize our activities.

3. We have a difficult time allowing ourselves to do nothing. We feel that every minute of our time must be productive.

3. We will practice taking short breaks throughout the day, allowing ourselves to do nothing.

4. Even when we're physically able to slow down, we often find that our thoughts are still racing.

4. We will try to slow down our thinking. If we can't, then we'll try to be okay with that.

5. We often feel like we're working within a time frame; we feel we must get on to the next task even before completing the task we're on.

5. We will focus on the task at hand, reminding ourselves that there's no need to rush ahead.

6. We think that the faster we go, the more efficient we are, and that moving slowly is a sign of laziness. This kind of thinking results in feelings of inadequacy.

6. It will help if we allow ourselves to slow down, reassuring ourselves that it is not a sign of inefficiency.

43

It's difficult for those of us who have an anxiety disorder to think that we can benefit in any way from our anxiety problem. We're usually well into recovery, or recovered, before we're able to look back and appreciate what we've learned from our experience. Laura took a good look at her lifestyle and realized that her fast pace had been causing some of her stress.

An author once wrote that agoraphobia was the best thing that ever happened to him. I'll have to admit that it has certainly made me more aware of how my lifestyle affects my anxiety level. I've always tried to take on more than one person would be expected to handle in one day, and, of course, I've had the highest expectations. I think that I have since managed to cut back on my busy lifestyle as well as my expectations of myself. Here is a list of some helpful changes that have come about because of my experience with an anxiety disorder:

1. *I try to tackle one project at a time, seeing it through to the end, rather than take on several projects at once.*
2. *I give myself extra time when getting ready to go somewhere, rather than wait until the last minute. If I don't have the extra time, I try to give myself permission to be late rather than feel rushed.*
3. *I make a list of things that I want to accomplish. Once the item is on the list, I know that it will eventually get done. I try not to put a time limit on it if possible. If I check off only one item at the end of the day, it's okay.*
4. *I try to move at a slower pace rather than meet myself coming and going by running in circles.*
5. *I give myself permission to take breaks. It used to be, if I had fifteen extra minutes on my hands I'd fill in the time with something I felt had to be done. Now I sometimes choose to do nothing.*
6. *I try to see more options in my life. I figure I have a choice of scrubbing my kitchen floor or going for a walk. Either activity is fine, but it's my choice.*

7. I try to exercise several times a week, making it fun, like taking a dance class, riding my bike, or swimming.

8. Sometimes, when I'm aware that my muscles are especially tense, I allow myself to let go of the tension and practice diaphragmatic breathing. I especially like to do this while waiting in traffic or sitting behind my desk at work.

9. I try to give myself permission to make mistakes without feeling bad about myself or giving myself a hard time.

10. I try to allow all thoughts and feelings without passing judgment on them.

11. I try to spend a little time each day giving of myself, and then I spend a little time doing for myself.

STRATEGY 5

A. Managing Our Anxiety: Letting Go of Control

With the onset of intense anxiety or panic, our first reaction is to try to stay in control. It will help if we practice letting go; the less we attempt to stay in control, the more in control we will feel.

Control is a major issue for those of us with an anxiety problem. Often feeling anxious, and therefore vulnerable, we are constantly on guard against losing control. Loss of control can mean having a panic attack; leaving a situation because of panic, generalized anxiety, dizziness, or light-headedness; experiencing a feeling of unreality; and, strangely enough, even feeling calm and relaxed. Whichever form it takes, we perceive loss of control as unacceptable. We fear that losing control will lead to a shameful conclusion that will intensify our sense of personal inadequacy.

A panic attack can seem like the ultimate in loss of control. We just aren't sure where it's going to take us or what might be waiting for us on the other side of the panic. We tell ourselves that we must do something to stop it. The most logical way, of course, would be to take control of it. However, there is nothing logical about panic attacks. The message "I must stay in control" is not very effective and usually results in the very panic attack we're trying so hard to avoid. As illogical as it seems, the best way to "control" a panic attack is not to control it at all. In other words, the more we can let go and allow it to happen, the less likely the panic will occur. We are especially on the alert when we approach a situation in which we've panicked before. Of course, there is nothing unrealistic about expecting to panic in such situations.

Dizziness and light-headedness can also give us the feeling of being out of control. Often we fear they will lead to fainting. Rather than taking the chance of attracting that kind of attention, we avoid going to public places where we think that might happen. We feel particularly vulnerable when the symptoms have persisted over a long period of time.

Our interpretation of what we think might be happening can be very frightening, triggering more anxiety and feelings of loss of control. What might be helpful is to give ourselves a simple explanation: *I'm feeling very anxious today. Perhaps I need to slow down.* Or, *Maybe I'm hyperventilating.* We then need to let go of trying to control the anxiety and give it all the room it needs; in other words, to just let it happen. We might encourage the thought *This is who I am today,* or *This is how I'm feeling right now,* and then allow ourselves to muddle through the best we can. Not trying to control the symptoms can help free us from feeling trapped.

A feeling of unreality is one of the most challenging symptoms to cope with. It is very frightening because we believe we are losing our sanity. But such feelings are not dangerous. If we can leave them alone, reassuring ourselves that they are harmless, they too will pass.

Escaping an uncomfortable situation also gives us a feeling of losing control, since we interpret it as a signal of a complete breakdown in coping skills. We tell ourselves, *If I can't stay right here and deal with this, it will get the better of me. It will continue to get worse, and I'll lose complete control over this whole situation.* Sooner or later we learn that giving ourselves permission to leave actually helps us to stay.

It makes sense that anxiety and panic can give us the feeling of being out of control, yet so can feeling calm and relaxed. Being relaxed can be uncomfortable for those of us with an anxiety problem, because we feel a need to be always on the alert for danger. We perceive tension as necessary, feeling that it is better to be tense and vigilant than to be caught off guard. It would help us if we could see that there's no need to be constantly anxious, just as there's no need to be constantly relaxed.

B. Listening to Our Inner Dialogue: Controlling/Letting Go

We believe that losing control is shameful and must be prevented, and that one way to do so is to keep tight control over our feelings and thoughts. We believe that losing control has catastrophic consequences. We believe that being in control not only averts disaster but helps keep us in a state that is beyond reproach. We're afraid that if we allow ourselves to be anxious, the anxiety will become unmanageable; we'll panic, and the panic might last forever. We tell ourselves that if we can control ourselves, we won't get anxious. However, just the opposite is true. The more we let go of control, the more in control we will feel.

A-Talk: Controlling	*B-Talk: Letting Go*
1. I must not let this get out of hand! I've got to stay in control!	1. I'll try to allow myself to let go of control. The more I can let go, the better.
2. I've got to keep on top of things! I can't allow myself to give in to this problem!	2. The more I try to stay on top of this, the more of a problem it's going to be.
3. I have to be cautious or else the anxiety might suddenly catch me off guard!	3. It will help if I try to let go, since it seems like the more cautious I am, the more anxious I get.
4. I can't relax! If I relax, things might get out of hand.	4. It's okay to relax! If things should get out of hand, so be it!
5. I can't go. If I do, I might lose control and make a fool of myself.	5. The fear of making a fool of myself is only a thought. Chances are, it's not going to happen.
6. I can't leave because of these feelings. If I give in to them now, it will be just that much worse the next time!	6. I do have the option to leave, in which case I could practice being okay with leaving. Knowing that I have that option will make it easier to stay, now or any other time.

C. Lifestyle Awareness: Letting Go of Control in Our Lives

We are aware that we sometimes feel out of control of our lives, which can leave us feeling trapped and helpless. We will try to let go, allow for more spontaneity, and see ourselves as having options.

Raising Our Level of Awareness

1. We sometimes feel out of control in relationships in which we perceive others as being in control, e.g., in the workplace.

1. Even though we might feel out of control, it will help if we try to do whatever we can to promote our sense of adequacy.

2. Our excessive need to be in control makes it difficult for us to take risks and to make changes in our lives. It promotes passivity and avoidance. Because we usually don't see ourselves as having options, we feel trapped and helpless.

2. Seeing ourselves as having options will help us reassure ourselves that we can take risks to bring about necessary changes. This will help us feel more in control of our lives.

3. We have a difficult time in situations where we really don't have control, e.g., as a passenger in a car or airplane.

3. We will try to let go and place more trust in others when we are in situations where we have no control.

4. When things do not work out the way we want them to, we tell ourselves we have to bring them under control.

4. It will help if we allow some situations to fall outside our perceived control. Where there is little we can do, it helps to let go.

The shopping mall is one of the biggest challenges for the phobic person because of its size and minimal access to doors. Kathy shares her experience of crossing the center court while shopping at a mall. As she felt the first wave of panic, her first thought was to try to stay in control. Kathy was able to deal with her panic attack by letting go and not trying to control it.

When I was in therapy, I learned the importance of not fighting the panic, not trying to control it, but just letting it happen. I'll never forget the first time I tried this strategy. I was at the mall. My husband and I were walking across the center court when I felt the first wave of panic. By the time we reached the other side I was fast approaching a ten on the panic scale. My first thought was, Oh, my God, I'm going to pass out! *I tried hard to stay in control of the situation. Reminding myself that what I was dealing with was only the thought of passing out, I immediately switched over to the thought,* This is only a panic attack. Go ahead and have it. If you're going to pass out, then just let yourself go, right here in the mall! *Within seconds the panic subsided and it was as though it hadn't happened. I couldn't have been more surprised! I stood there, absolutely amazed that feelings that had been so intense could subside so quickly. As a recovered agoraphobic, I look back on this as the beginning of the end.*

A. Managing Our Anxiety: Taking Risks

We will try to take risks rather than continually avoid places and situations where we feel anxious. It will help if we reassure ourselves that we are not in any danger and that we can function well even when we're uncomfortable.

Difficult as it may be, the best way to get through the panic is to actually go through it. We need to develop confidence in our coping skills, to know that we can make it through a panic attack, and that in spite of its intensity we can still function. Sometimes this means putting ourselves in situations where we might feel vulnerable to intense anxiety. It means taking risks.

Although risk-taking is a necessary part of our recovery, we manage to come up with any number of reasons for avoiding places where we might feel anxious or experience panic. The problem with avoidance is that our anxiety usually gets worse rather than better. Not wanting to take risks, we avoid more and more places, and our world progressively grows smaller. When we realize this is happening, we try to hold our ground so that our problem does not worsen. But this only causes more anxiety.

Unfortunately, not taking risks perpetuates this pattern of avoidance and keeps us stuck. So why do we avoid? For one thing, we're afraid that exposure to a feared situation could result in a serious setback. We think that having a bad experience might discourage us from trying again. Some of us feel that it could precipitate a physical reaction that would damage our health. Whatever the reason, we see avoidance as a form of protection.

Another reason for avoiding—one we might not be as aware of—is that we do not want to deal with the feeling of failure we experience when our anxiety becomes unmanageable and we feel that we have to leave the situation. In order to protect our self-esteem, we avoid taking the risk altogether.

Whatever our reason for avoiding, there is a way out of this panic-avoidance cycle. First, we need to give ourselves options, such as telling ourselves *It's okay to stay* and *It's okay to leave.* And then we need to see each risk as an opportunity to practice.* When we do take risks, we expect ourselves to perform perfectly, which sets us up for failure. Seeing each risk as continued practice diminishes our perception of failure.

For example, we can practice taking the risk of going out, allowing any anxiety we might have, going through a panic attack, and then staying in spite of the panic attack or accepting our decision to leave. We can also try to feel okay about ourselves when doing so. Viewing each of these options as an opportunity to practice, we can see that there is little or no possibility of failure.

At first, we might need the help of a support person, someone we feel safe with. As we gain confidence, we can begin venturing out on our own. As we gradually open ourselves to more risk-taking, we begin to realize that we can function even though we're feeling uncomfortable. It will help if we can allow ourselves to feel good about any risks we've taken regardless of the outcome (even though this is difficult for us to do).

As long as we feel that we are in some kind of danger, and as long as we insist on comfort or see the need to escape as failure, we will continue to avoid. Realizing that we do have choices in difficult situations, and seeing each situation as an opportunity to practice, can give us the confidence we need to take the risks that are necessary for recovery.

B. Listening to Our Inner Dialogue: Avoidance/Exposure
Avoidance has been a favorite strategy of ours in dealing with difficult problems. We seem to believe that avoiding problems is a way of getting rid of them and thus feeling less shame. However, avoidance strategies are harmful because they obscure problems, which then never get attended to. Especially troublesome is our avoidance of

---

* Dr. Claire Weekes discusses the concept of practice in her book *Hope and Help for Your Nerves* (New York: Bantam). She refers to it as "practice versus testing."

fearful thoughts. It explains, in part, why we find it difficult to make sense of our anxiety problems and our phobias. Avoidance also diminishes our self-esteem, since we perceive ourselves as unable to cope with everyday living.

A-Talk: Avoidance	*B-Talk: Exposure*
1. If I go, it will only make me feel anxious and my condition will get worse.	1. I might feel worse at first, but it's the avoidance, not the risking, that aggravates my anxiety problem.
2. I'm just not going. That way I won't have to deal with the anxiety or the feeling of failure if I should have to leave.	2. I don't have to go, but I'll probably feel bad about avoiding a difficult situation. Either way it will be good practice in dealing with my decision.
3. Maybe I'll go. I'll just tough it out. I'll put my mind on something else and try not to think about how I'm feeling!	3. Rather than trying to distract myself, I might find it more helpful to stay in touch with how I'm feeling.
4. I don't ever want to feel this way again!	4. I might not want to feel anxious again, but I most likely will. It will help if I can be accepting of that.
5. I'm leaving! I'm getting out of here before I have a full-blown panic attack!	5. It's okay to leave. I can practice being accepting of that. I don't have to stay in a difficult situation.
6. I can't leave. If I do, I'll be giving in to my fear, and it will be even more difficult to come back the next time.	6. Giving myself an out so that I don't feel trapped will make it easier to come back next time. I can even plan my escape. What matters is that I accept my decision.

C. Lifestyle Awareness: Facing Difficult Situations

We are aware that we often choose avoidance as a way of dealing with difficult situations. It would be more helpful to try to work through these difficulties. If we cannot bring about a change, it will help if we try to generate a new perception of the situation so that we will not feel trapped or helpless.

Raising Our Level of Awareness

1. We often express our feelings through silence to avoid confrontations with others. We see this as a way of keeping the peace and protecting our self-esteem from unnecessary attack.

1. We need to work through difficult situations by expressing how we feel rather than pretending the feelings don't exist or convincing ourselves that they don't matter. (This might require the help of a therapist or marriage counselor.)

2. We often avoid being assertive when we need to be. Assertiveness is difficult for those of us who feel we need the approval of others and do not want to rock the boat.

2. We can risk asserting ourselves in situations where we feel it might be helpful. This might mean expressing our opinion at the expense of keeping the peace.

3. We often do not see ourselves as having options, which gives us a feeling of being stuck, trapped, or helpless.

3. It would help if we could see the possibility of choices when dealing with difficult situations. If we cannot bring about a change, we might try to generate a new perception of our situation so that we will not feel trapped or helpless.

Taking it one step at a time can be an effective way of approaching a scary situation. Strategies such as slowing down and focusing on the moment can help us deal with our anxiety when taking risks.

> *My husband and I were invited to a rock concert. I really wanted to go! I knew, of course, that I couldn't. So I spent the next two weeks going crazy. My inner dialogue went something like this: I really want to go, but I can't, and since I can't, I must be a failure. I felt extremely tense because of this. The morning of the concert my anxiety was really bad. On a scale of one to ten, my anxiety was at about a nine. So I called another support group member. She said something that really helped me. She told me that when she wanted to go out, she would just put herself in the car and go, taking it one step at a time and thinking of it as practice. I decided to do the same thing. Rather than thinking of it in*

terms of going to the concert, I focused on the moment. First, I put myself in the shower. Then, I got myself ready. Not only did I take it step by step, but I thought only about what I was doing at the time. I also asked my husband if he would leave anytime I asked him. I felt better about that. I felt I had some control. It wasn't until I put myself in the car that I knew that I was really going to the concert. Looking back, I can see that I was focusing on and enjoying the moment, rather than anticipating horrors (which never came). For the rest of the evening I just had fun. It was having fun that was so important. I knew I could white-knuckle it through almost anything; I had done it many times. But this time, I was actually having fun! I really felt good afterward. Having had a successful experience attending the concert has given me hope. It happened once, and with continued practice, I know that it will happen again.

—DENISE

A. Managing Our Anxiety: Allowing Catastrophic Thoughts

When catastrophizing with the what-ifs, we will try to be permissive of them and not fight them. It will help to realize that they are only thoughts and that chances are they will not happen. It might also help to affirm that we carry our safety within.

Anyone who is chronically anxious or has ever had a panic attack is familiar with the what-ifs. With the slightest indication of anxiety we are quick to ask ourselves, *What if this anxiety becomes unmanageable? What if I panic? What if I faint? What if I make a fool of myself?* Catastrophic thoughts are not uncommon. Everyone has them at one time or another. However, they are usually taken in stride. Those of us with anxiety problems, on the other hand, perceive them as omens of disaster and feel we have to get rid of them. It is important for us to know that there is nothing wrong with having catastrophic thoughts and that we do not have to do anything about them. It's only when we perceive them as a problem that they become a problem.

When dealing with catastrophic thoughts, two strategies might help: (1) perceiving the catastrophic thought as normal and acceptable, and (2) making use of the catastrophic thought as an opportunity to figure out what we might do to get through a feared situation before we're actually faced with it. For instance:

Q. What if I faint?

A. I've never fainted before and chances are it's not going to happen now. If it does, someone will help me. I hate the thought of fainting, but that's all it is—a thought.

Q. What if I get anxious while I'm driving and get into an accident?

A. This is only a thought about causing an accident. If I get anxious, I will try to go with the feeling. I can always pull over if the anxiety becomes unmanageable.

Dealing with persistent and unexplainable symptoms, and at times a sense of impending doom, is it any wonder that we become concerned about them and ask what if? We will most likely experience a lot of panic attacks before we are reassured that the what-ifs are unlikely to happen.

It can help if we allow the catastrophic thoughts to be there, while at the same time encouraging an inner dialogue that is in direct competition with them. Being permissive of catastrophic thoughts will diminish their troublesome nature.

We might gently affirm that we carry our safety within, that our safety is not back home or in any other given place, and that what we are experiencing is only a feeling. This will not be easy at first, but the thought itself might help keep us from frightening ourselves further.

What-ifs are not always questions about what to do. For instance, when we ask, *What if I panic?* we're not necessarily asking what we should do in case of a panic attack. What we're actually saying is *I must not panic* or *I've got to control the panic.* At this point it doesn't really help to become rational. What helps is to try seeing the thought of panicking as acceptable.

Catastrophic thoughts will probably continue, but hopefully to a less troublesome degree. It will help if we are patient with the what-ifs, allowing them to be there and realizing that they are normal. Catastrophic thoughts are not about real events; they are thoughts that encourage us to prepare ourselves to cope with anticipated events before they actually occur.

B. Listening to Our Inner Dialogue: Distracting/Inviting
Fearful thoughts and catastrophic thoughts are honest-to-goodness emotions. We don't need to alter, change, control, or get rid of them—nor could we if we wanted to. Rather than presenting a problem, they can actually serve a purpose. If we listen to what they tell us, we can become better prepared for anticipated events that are scaring us. For example, we can engage in some anticipatory problem-solving, which will help us cope better.

A-Talk: Distracting

B-Talk: Inviting

1. I'll try to put my mind on something else! I'm just not going to allow these thoughts anymore!

1. Trying to distract myself doesn't always work very well. Besides, they're only thoughts. It helps if I allow them to be there.

2. I've got to stop worrying so much!

2. I'll start worrying less when I stop trying so hard to control my thoughts. It might help if I see worry as an option, and see that it sometimes serves a purpose.

3. I have to stop thinking this way!

3. Telling myself that I have to stop these thoughts only makes matters worse.

4. I shouldn't have these thoughts. There must be something terribly wrong with me for thinking this way.

4. They're only thoughts. It's okay to have them! It doesn't mean that there's something terribly wrong with me.

5. What if my worst fear really does happen? I'd better make sure it doesn't!

5. So be it! I'll deal with it the best I can when the time comes.

C. LIFESTYLE AWARENESS: ALLOWING UNWANTED THOUGHTS

We are aware that our tendency to catastrophize makes it difficult to be receptive to positive outcomes. It will help if we are permissive of our thoughts, both positive and negative, rather than feeling that we have to block them out or replace them with other thoughts.

Raising Our Level of Awareness

1. Worrying can sometimes give us a feeling of having control over an otherwise out-of-control situation. Sometimes we feel that by worrying we can actually keep bad things from happening.

1. It will help if we realize that we cannot control future events by worrying about them. However, we will try to allow worry as an option, since not allowing worry—fearful that it might get out of hand—is the same as not allowing thoughts.

2. We sometimes worry to a point where it no longer seems helpful. We just don't know when to let go of it.

2. It will help if we realize that there is a point where we can let go of worry: when we have worried over a long period of time, when the worry is about something that is completely out of our control, or when it's about an event in the distant future.

3. Positive thinking can be challenging for those of us who are phobic and/or depressed. When we have difficulty conjuring up positive thoughts to replace the negative ones, we feel that we have failed and that there must be something terribly wrong with us.

3. Realizing that it is difficult to simply replace a negative thought, we might think in terms of being more receptive to positive thoughts, seeing them as options and not as "have-tos." It will help if we can feel okay about ourselves when positive thoughts are difficult to come by.

4. We tend to resist unwanted thoughts by trying to block them out or by frantically trying to replace them with other thoughts.

4. It will help if we allow all thoughts, even those that seem troublesome, rather than blocking them out or doing battle with them. We will try to see them for what they are—just thoughts.

Debby's testimonial tells us how her B-talk helped her deal with her catastrophic thoughts. Her self-talk, along with an understanding and acceptance of her agoraphobia, helped her take the risk of driving to the airport.

I was going to take a friend of mine to the airport. We decided to eat dinner first at a Chinese restaurant. After dinner I began to feel anxious about the drive. I told my friend my fears, and he asked if I wanted to go home. I really didn't. I really wanted to take him to the airport. (Lately, the risks have been more important than the symptoms. It's a new feeling for me and it feels great!)

I drove to the airport, figuring I could work out some of the anxiety before I had to travel back alone. It was great! I knew I was dealing with agoraphobia and not everyday anxiety. I am now distinguishing between the two and allowing myself to experience them. My drive home by myself was good (for an agoraphobic). It was normal for what I expected. I listened to my B-talk; I reminded myself that I could wave someone down to help me—people do help other people. I could always pull over or get to a phone and call someone; it really isn't that far. I told myself that the drive would soon be over (rather than thinking it would never be over). I repeated to myself, Thoughts of passing out, getting sick, or whatever, are really just thoughts. I've had them before. What else is new? I will get through this. I'm glad I am doing this. It is part of my recovery process.

I was tired when I got home, but not exhausted. I am learning to be good to myself.

Dealing with agoraphobia has become a lifetime goal. I am learning to accept and love that part of me. I see this acceptance as part of my recovery process.

A. Managing Our Anxiety: Learning and Talking About Our Anxiety Disorder

We will try to develop a more helpful attitude toward our anxiety disorder by learning more about it, thus removing the veil of mystery. By talking about it, we also lift the burden of a deep, dark secret.

The fear we experience during an anxiety or panic episode is especially alarming because we do not know what is happening to us. Unfortunately, most of the explanations we come up with on our own frighten us even more, and we do one of two things: either we avoid learning anything about our problem, or we seek excessively complex explanations, which causes us to become more frustrated. In both cases we're unable to come up with simple and accurate answers.

The more inquisitive we are about our anxiety or panic attacks, and the more we learn about our disorder, the less alarmed we will be by its apparent mysteries. Just knowing that our problem has a name helps, but all too often our knowledge stops there. It's not uncommon to hear such statements as "Perhaps the less I hear about this the better," or, "I'm afraid that if I read about this problem, I'll pick up new symptoms and continue to get worse." This is just one more way of avoiding. It's like saying, "If I don't think about my anxiety, it will go away." Unfortunately, it doesn't work that way.

Taking away the mystery will help alleviate the fear. We might begin by seeing an anxiety or panic attack as an interesting phenomenon that comes from within, one that we ourselves have set into motion with our thoughts, rather than seeing it as a frightening attack that comes from out of the blue, leaving us bewildered and out of control.

Learning about our anxiety and panic removes much of the mystery. Many books and articles provide insight and suggestions for dealing with anxiety disorders. It will help if we approach our quest for knowledge gradually, without the attitude of "I have to get over this problem once and for all." What is important is to open ourselves to information about our problem and to be willing to risk learning more about it.

Discussing our anxiety disorder with others is difficult, since we're not really sure ourselves what's happening. Unfortunately, whenever we carry a deep, dark secret we take on the extra burden of shame, which only adds to our anxiety. Our inner dialogue is permeated with such thoughts as *I shouldn't feel this way, Something is terribly wrong with me,* and *What will people think?* If we haven't come to terms with the fact that we have an anxiety disorder, how can we possibly discuss it with others who have little idea of what we're talking about and who, we feel, might stand in judgment of us?

At the same time, it isn't necessary to rush into the boss's office the first day on the job and announce that we are prone to intense anxiety or panic attacks that seem to come out of nowhere at the most inappropriate times. We might begin by confiding in a spouse or close friend. Being somewhat casual or matter-of-fact about our situation can help put the listener at ease. For instance, when having lunch with a friend, we might say, "I sometimes feel panicky in restaurants. So if I step out for a minute, you don't have to worry." If our attitude says that it's no big deal, chances are that the other person will see it that way too. Being able to talk about our anxiety disorder as just another fact of life tends to make it just that.

Trying to see our situation in humorous terms can also help put things into better perspective. It is possible to find humor in having driven thirty miles out of the way to avoid an expressway or having climbed seven flights of stairs to avoid taking an elevator. If we could not laugh at our plight, its reality would be overwhelming.

B. Listening to Our Inner Dialogue: Avoidance/Exposure

Avoiding an understanding of how our problem works can be very appealing, but usually the problem only becomes mysterious and alarming. On the other hand, trying to understand and analyze the problem too deeply can be an exercise in continuous frustration. Perhaps our goal can be to arrive at a simple and accurate understanding of what is troubling us.

A-Talk: Avoidance

1. It would be better not to read anything about this problem, or it might get worse.

2. I don't want to hear anyone else talk about this, because I just might pick up their symptoms.

3. If I just don't think about it, the problem will eventually go away.

4. If people find out about this, they're going to think there's something wrong with me.

5. It's best that I don't talk about this to anyone, because of what people might think.

B-Talk: Exposure

1. My problem might get worse for a while, but that's only because I'm facing it and trying to deal with it.

2. While it's possible for me to pick up symptoms, it's better to take that risk than to keep running away from the problem.

3. Trying not to think about my problem doesn't seem to help. As a matter of fact, the more I try not to think about it, the worse it gets.

4 My *real* concern is how I might *feel* about people having that thought about me. I'll try to feel okay about myself regardless of what others think about me.

5. It might help to open up to a close friend, someone I can trust. The more I try to hide this, the more anxious I seem to feel.

C. Lifestyle Awareness: Understanding Events in Our Lives

We are aware that we sometimes avoid processing difficult events in our lives by not thinking about them or by distorting their meaning. It will help if we take a good look at them and try to see the meaning they have for us.

Raising Our Level of Awareness

1. We often avoid processing difficult events in our lives by not thinking about them. For example, if we are having a conflict with someone at work, we avoid trying to understand what the conflict is about and therefore avoid finding ways to resolve it.

1. It would help if we took a good look at difficult events in our lives, understood what they were about, and tried to resolve them.

2. If something bothers us, we often distort its meaning or try not to think about it so that it no longer bothers us.

2. Rather than explaining a problem to ourselves in a way that completely distorts its meaning, it is much more helpful to explain it in a way that makes simple sense of it and then accept it for what it is.

3. We often experience considerable stress when a problem arises, but we resort to relieving the symptoms of stress rather than face the events that are creating it.

3. It would be helpful to allow ourselves to feel the physical manifestations of stress while trying to attend to its cause.

It is not uncommon to experience symptoms when reading about our anxiety problem. Many of us can identify with Ken's dilemma of wanting to learn more about his phobia but being afraid to do so for fear of becoming more anxious.

> *For a long time I didn't know what was going on with me. I couldn't figure out how other people could just get in their cars and drive anywhere they wanted—I had such an awful time getting to the corner store. The constant anxiety and unpredictable panic attacks were a mystery to me. Since I was too embarrassed to tell my family or my friends about my problem, I felt pretty much cut off from everyone.*
>
> *I decided to read up on anxiety and panic disorders and got a book on the subject. But as I paged through it, the symptoms it described hit too close to home. I felt more anxious than ever and*

questioned whether I should be reading it. It seemed better to just not think about my problem. So halfway through the first chapter, I put the book in a drawer, where it remained for some time.

Later, in therapy, I learned that the more curious I could become about phobias the better. So I decided to chance it again. I got a book on agoraphobia. I even found a tape about a recovered agoraphobic. I have to admit that learning more about my problem has helped. The panic attacks aren't quite as scary anymore. What's more, I can pretty much read about anxiety and panic without much of a problem. At times, it still makes me a little uneasy, but I guess I'm okay with that.

A. Managing Our Anxiety: Keeping Our Expectations Low

When approaching a situation where we feel anxious, we will try to take it one step at a time, keeping our expectations low. It will help if we think of it as an opportunity to practice.

Just as we tend to expect ourselves to do well in general, we also expect to do well when we are in situations where we feel anxious. By setting our expectations high (and not allowing for any discomfort), we believe that we will raise our level of performance. However, just the opposite is true. When we raise our expectations, we only add more anxiety to an already distressed system. On the other hand, the less we expect to do well, the less pressure we put on ourselves and the more efficiently we'll be able to perform. In other words, the more we can allow ourselves *not* to do well, the better we'll do.

We tend to set high expectations in situations such as returning to a place where we had done particularly well. We feel that because we handled our anxiety well the last time, we should be able to do as well again, if not better. The same holds true for traveling. If the outbound trip went well, we expect the return trip to go well too. With our expectations up, however, the least sign of discomfort can trigger intense anxiety. What happens the second time around is that we automatically raise our expectations of doing well. It will help if we see each experience as practice and continue to lower our expectations by allowing ourselves to be uncomfortable. We forget that the reason we coped well before was that we lowered our expectations. Having forgotten that, the A-talk returns and we are convinced that the repeat event should be a piece of cake. The pressure generated by such high expectations causes us to respond to the slightest discomfort with great alarm. During these times we are most vulnerable to panic attacks, exactly when we least expect them. It is when we expect the panic attacks to happen and allow the anticipation that we cope the best and that panic attacks are the least likely to occur.

As perfectionists, we expect not only a high score in handling our anxiety but a complete recovery—as soon as possible. Unfortunately, the more effort we put forth, the more frustrated we become. Here again, we need to lower our expectations and allow as much time as necessary for recovery. If we can reassure ourselves that we will be able to manage and that our difficulties with anxiety will improve with time, we may feel less trapped in a situation that once seemed unmanageable.

So as we approach each situation where we feel anxious, it will help if we try to take it one step at a time, keeping our expectations low and allowing for any discomfort. Seeing the situation as an opportunity to practice will help us in our recovery.

B. LISTENING TO OUR INNER DIALOGUE: RAISING/LOWERING EXPECTATIONS

We tend to think that the way to deal with any problem is to raise expectations as much as possible: the higher our expectations, the better we'll be able to solve a problem. We believe that if we set 100 percent success as a minimum expectation, we'll be more likely to cope with maximum efficiency. Failure must be prevented at all costs, because failure is shameful and therefore unacceptable. Moreover, we believe that the more we fail, the more unmanageable our problem will become. Thus we believe we should do our best to avoid failure. It might seem paradoxical, but the more we lower our expectations and allow for failure, the less anxiety we'll experience and the better we'll do.

A-Talk: Raising Expectations	*B-Talk: Lowering Expectations*
1. I must not get anxious. I must not fail again!	1. Chances are, I will be anxious. However, the more I can allow the anxiety, the better. It will help if I can see this as a chance to practice having these feelings, rather than as a failure.
2. I did well the last time I was here, so this should be easy.	2. Sometimes it's more difficult the next time out, because I automatically raise my expectations. It will help if I can continue to keep my expectations low.

A-Talk: Raising Expectations	*B-Talk: Lowering Expectations*
3. I should try harder!	3. Sometimes it's best to let up a little and not try so hard, since the harder I try, the worse it seems to get.
4. I must not escape to avoid this anxiety or it will be that much more difficult to come back the next time.	4. It's important to take risks, but telling myself that I have to stay only makes me feel trapped. If I give myself the option to leave, it might make it easier for me to come back the next time.
5. If I can't do it well, I shouldn't even try.	5. It doesn't have to be great—or even good. Just taking the risk is helpful.
6. If I'm not succeeding, it's because I'm not trying hard enough!	6. If I'm not succeeding, it might be because I'm trying too hard. Sometimes it's best to do nothing and just muddle through.

C. LIFESTYLE AWARENESS: ALLOWING IMPERFECTION

We are aware of our need for perfectionism. It will help if we allow ourselves to be average rather than continually strive for perfection. We might remind ourselves that making mistakes does not have to affect our self-worth.

Raising Our Level of Awareness

1. Our perfectionism may be a sign of low self-esteem. As children we may have been denied the freedom to fail.	1. We can try to lower our expectations and allow for failure. It will help if we see failure as an opportunity for growth.
2. Our perfectionism can sometimes be a result of trying to make up for what we perceive to be defective in us. We feel that making a mistake contributes to a further loss of self-esteem.	2. It helps if we realize that our desire to be perfect can be self-defeating. In other words, the harder we try, the more inefficient we'll become.
3. We impose high standards on ourselves; if we do not live up to them, we feel our self-worth will diminish.	3. We can try to develop more reasonable or manageable expectations. We might even challenge ourselves to be average rather than continually striving for perfection.

4. We are fearful that we might panic in a crisis.	4. It might help to remind ourselves that we usually function well in a crisis situation, since our expectations at that time are lowered.

When going into a feared situation, we often test ourselves to see how well we can do. With our expectations high, however, we react to the slightest sign of discomfort. Julie discovered that she could actually enjoy shopping at a mall on a busy holiday weekend by lowering her expectations of how well she would do.

Shopping the day after Thanksgiving has long been on my avoidance list. The closest I could get to the mall, even under ordinary circumstances, would be to drop my mother and daughters off to shop on their own and retreat to the safety of my home. Just driving into the parking lot was enough to bring on a feeling of panic. But since I've learned some coping skills, things have certainly changed. After venturing into the mall this past Thanksgiving weekend, I feel I've really made progress. It wasn't easy! When I started out, my mind was full of scary thoughts. However, I allowed them to be there, reassuring myself that they were only thoughts. Once at the mall, I kept my expectations low. I didn't expect to feel absolutely anxiety-free while making my way through crowds of shoppers. I allowed the uneasiness that I occasionally experienced while moving through the crowded stores. I simply was not impressed with any of these feelings. I took my time. Even though my shopping list was long, my goal was to buy just one item, if that. This automatically took the rush out of my day. I also gave myself permission to leave if necessary. I found myself enjoying the sights and sounds of Christmas and marveled at the fact that I was a part of all the pre-Christmas activity there at the mall—a first in a long time. During this Thanksgiving season I am truly filled with gratitude!

❧

A. Managing Our Anxiety: Accepting Setbacks

We will try to accept setbacks as a normal and necessary part of our recovery, trying to see them as temporary. It might help to remind ourselves that even though we feel as if we're starting over, we never really go back to square one.

The recovery process is never smooth. We seem to do well for a while, and then suddenly the rug is pulled out from under us. What might have been easy yesterday is difficult today. Just when we thought that we were finally getting better, those all-too-familiar feelings of intense anxiety or panic seem to come out of nowhere. Our self-talk reverts to *Oh, no, not again! I'm never going to get over this! I'm right back where I started!* Along with having feelings of failure and discouragement, we're consumed with the fear that we are in a continuous cycle of being out of control and there is nothing we can do about it.

The fear of being out of control of our faculties is a particularly disturbing part of setbacks. Not only do we feel extremely vulnerable, but the what-ifs abound: *What if this sets in for good? What if it continues to get worse?* and so on. We try hard to eliminate the catastrophic thoughts. Our inclination is to hang on tight, stay in control, and hold our ground to avoid backtracking. What might be helpful at this point, however, is to do just the opposite: give ourselves permission not to be in control, and even to lose some ground if necessary. It will help if we remind ourselves that in spite of a feeling of losing ground, we will not go back to square one and we are still making progress. The truth is, we never really go back to where we started; it only seems that way because we've had a short reprieve and felt like a "regular" person again. And now the situation seems worse by comparison. Besides, how can we possibly go back to square one when we've learned so much about our problem and how to deal with it? Our perception is beginning to change, and it can never be quite the same as it was when we first started experiencing panic attacks.

It helps to know that there are reasons for setbacks. Usually they signal the need to slow down. On days when we're feeling good and we're able to get out to do some of the things we haven't been able to do for a while, we tend to overdo it, which leaves us feeling depleted. Also, when all has gone well for a while, our expectations go up and we might tell ourselves, *Well, I did this last week and had no problem. This should be a piece of cake.* When we have such high expectations and do not allow for any discomfort, the least sign of a symptom can throw us into a whirlwind of anxiety or panic. Whether we leave or stay matters little. We feel as though we've failed once again, and the feeling of being out of control becomes demoralizing.

How we perceive or interpret our setbacks can make a difference in how troublesome they are or how long they last. Seeing them as isolated events rather than continuous chain reactions can help take away some of the fear that they are setting in for good. Our self-talk might be, *This is today. It has no bearing on what will happen tomorrow,* or *This too shall pass.* We might wish to remind ourselves that setbacks are a normal and necessary part of our recovery. We might even see them as opportunities for continued practice in working through the anxiety or panic attacks. The more we practice being permissive of the panic feelings, the less frightening they become and the more confidence we gain in working with them. We have learned to frighten ourselves. It will take time to relearn a new kind of inner dialogue, one that is reassuring and supportive. As we approach each new plateau, we can remind ourselves that the setback is a transition period that allows us to make continued progress.

B. LISTENING TO OUR INNER DIALOGUE:
NONACCEPTANCE/ACCEPTANCE

Setbacks are normal. They are opportunities to practice dealing with difficult situations. Since it's impossible to get well without setbacks, it's important that we have them. But when we do have them, it feels as if we're back to square one. In reality, setbacks are preludes to progressive phases. When we have setbacks, it helps if we let them be, not trying so hard to get rid of them or control them, but letting them take their natural course. Before we know it, they subside, and we are on our way to making more progress.

A-Talk: Nonacceptance	B-Talk: Acceptance
1. I'm never going to get over this. I'm right back where I started!	1. This gets better, but it takes time. It helps if I can try to accept that. Although it may seem like I'm back where I started, I am making progress.
2. I can't afford to have this problem anymore. It has to stop right now!	2. Telling myself that it has to stop only makes matters worse. It's better to try to allow the anxiety to take its course.
3. Enough of this! I just can't take this anymore!	3. It's going to happen whether I want it to or not. It helps if I try to accept that.
4. I'm always going to be this way!	4. I'll try to be open to the thought that it might be this way for a long time. But it will improve.
5. I've just got to be normal!	5. What is normal? Everyone has a problem. Mine is having a difficult time dealing with unmanageable fear or panic attacks. So be it!
6. Why can't this problem just go away and never come back!	6. This isn't just coming from out of the blue. There's a reason why I'm having these feelings. It might help if I slow down or perhaps take a look at what's happening in my life that keeps me anxious.

C. LIFESTYLE AWARENESS: GIVING OURSELVES THE FREEDOM TO FAIL

We are aware that we have a difficult time dealing with failure, seeing it as further evidence of low self-worth. It will help if we give ourselves the freedom to fail, considering it an opportunity for growth.

Raising Our Level of Awareness

1. Our high standards of perfectionism do not readily allow for failure. We tend to see it as further proof of our inadequacies or defectiveness. We have to succeed at work, we have to be perfect parents, we must even excel at our hobbies.

1. It will help to generate the thought, *I don't have to succeed, and if I fail, that would provide me with a valuable learning experience.*

2. We tend to associate our self-worth with how well we perform. Rather than feeling bad about ourselves, we choose not to perform at all.

2. We might try to remind ourselves that anyone can feel good when he or she does well. The real challenge is to feel all right about ourselves when we don't do well.

3. Our fear of failure can keep us from taking risks and doing the things that we really want to do in life.

3. We will try to take more risks, allowing ourselves the freedom to fail, seeing it as an opportunity for growth. We might even imagine the worst that could happen and then allow for that possibility.

Setbacks can be alarming, but it will help if we try to accept them. In the following testimonial, Jerry talks about his setbacks and how he eventually accepted them and understood the reason for their recurrence.

> *I think the most difficult part of my recovery was going through setbacks. I dreaded them! I hated the discouragement and failure each time I went through one. I felt like I was starting over. I'd be feeling okay for a while, and the next thing I knew, I'd be white-knuckling my way into places where I had experienced no anxiety just the week before. It didn't make any sense! The worst part for me was feeling so out of control of my life. I felt helpless, like there was nothing I could do about the endlessly recurring anxiety and panic attacks.*
>
> *I guess I figured that once I stopped panicking I was cured. I*

could just go on with my life and not even think about it anymore. In retrospect, with my high expectations of doing well, falling back into my A-talk, and rushing through my day, why was I surprised when my anxiety returned?

My therapist told me, "It will happen whether you want it to or not." At first, this comment seemed callous. It really made me angry. But the more I thought about it, the more I came to accept the fact that setbacks were inevitable. I figured, if they were going to happen that automatically, I might as well not fight them. As time went on, the setbacks occurred less often with longer periods of time in between. I can see now that if I'd recovered quickly, I'd still wonder how it all happened and what I'd do if I should ever panic again. With all of my practice with setbacks, I've gained a lot of confidence in handling future panic attacks.

❧

STRATEGY 11

A. Managing Our Anxiety: Taking the Time Limit Out of Recovery

We will try to take the time limit out of our recovery, seeing it as open-ended. It will help if we try to accept where we are right now without comparing ourselves with past progress, and at the same time, try to be accepting of the possibility of any future anxiety.

Among the many fears we have as anxiety or panic sufferers, one is that our condition will set in for good and grow increasingly worse until we are totally out of control. We find ourselves making comparisons, reminding ourselves of all the things we used to be able to do and can't do now. We then continue to frighten ourselves with the thought of how much worse it might be in the future. It will help if we allow that thought to be there, and then remind ourselves to try to be more accepting of our situation as it was, as it is now, and as it might be.

Wanting a quick recovery, we tend to place a time limit on our progress. We tell ourselves, *I'd better be over this in six months,* and then we think, *But what if I'm not?* Unfortunately, a time limit slows down the recovery process by imposing restrictions on us and burdening us with more pressures. It can also give us a feeling of being trapped, which only adds to our anxiety.

Keeping it open-ended (not putting it into a time frame) can do much to alleviate this feeling of being trapped. It gives us more options. We can begin by slowing down. We no longer have to hurry to get better, since there's plenty of time and it's no longer an all-or-nothing situation. With an attitude of acceptance, we might tell ourselves, *This is who I am today. So be it.* We might try to see this as a time to reflect on what is happening in our lives that is causing so much distress; for instance, personal issues that we might be dealing with, or perhaps *not* dealing with.

It would help if we could take each day as it comes, accepting where we are right now in our recovery, without unduly analyzing, comparing, or judging. Going to bed at night unwilling to face the anxiety that might be there the next morning is a sure way to make it happen. The key is accepting that it probably will be there tomorrow, and for any number of mornings after that.

The possibility that our recovery will be a long process is very discouraging. However, we have learned that our anxiety and panic attacks are manageable and that we can still function in spite of them. When we lower our expectations and let time take care of itself, our difficulties with anxiety *will* get better, and we can be reassured that as life goes on, we will still be a part of it.

B. Listening to Our Inner Dialogue: Perfectionism/Nonperfectionism

When we're phobic, we perceive time in an extremely austere manner. We see it as something we need to control. We want to make certain that future events happen exactly the way we want them to. All this adds to our state of persistent self-aggravation. We would do much better if we allowed time and future events to take their natural course.

A-Talk: Perfectionism	*B-Talk: Nonperfectionism*
1. I'm always going to have this problem. It's never going to get any better!	1. It's only natural that I have this thought. It helps if I can see it as that—a thought! With time and patience, it does get better.
2. I'm afraid this will continue to get worse until I'm completely out of control!	2. It's true that it might get worse. In fact, at times it probably will. It helps if I can allow that to happen and remind myself that relapsing is a normal part of the recovery process.
3. If it's this bad now, how much worse will it be in six months?	3. How I'm feeling right now has no bearing on how I might feel six months from now. For all I know, I'll feel better tomorrow.

A-Talk: Perfectionism	*B-Talk: Nonperfectionism*
4. I used to be able to drive across the state. Now I can't even make it as far as the corner store.	4. With practice, I will be able to get to the store again, and I will be able to travel long distances as well.
5. I'd better be over this in six months. But what if I'm not?	5. It helps to think of my recovery as open-ended. Regardless of how long it takes, I will get better.
6. I can make it to the grocery store now, but I still can't drive on the expressway.	6. I'll give myself credit for being able to get to the grocery store, and try to be okay about not driving on the expressway. I'll drive on the expressway when I'm ready.

C. LIFESTYLE AWARENESS: LIVING ONE DAY AT A TIME

We are aware that it helps to live one day at a time, while slowly coming to terms with the past and letting the future take care of itself.

Raising Our Level of Awareness

1. Even though we know that we can't change the past, we tend not to accept troubling past events.	1. It will help if we try to work through past events that are troubling. When we accept them, we will be able to let go of them.
2. We can feel trapped by our past because we are unwilling to process the meanings it has for us. For example, we are often unwilling to make a connection between the trauma or abuse of our childhood and our problem with anxiety.	2. Rather than repressing these past experiences, we might find it helpful to try to see their relationship to the present.
3. We separate ourselves from the mainstream of life. We have a tendency to watch life go by, rather than actually becoming part of it.	3. We will try to spontaneously get into the course of our life without waiting for things to improve.

One of the most difficult things for us to do is to take recovery out of a time frame. It's so tempting to set goals for ourselves and think that we should be well within a given period of time. In the following testimonial, Greg discovered that the more time he gave himself, the better he felt.

When I started therapy, the first thing I told myself was, "I should be better in three months." Three months later, however, I was still struggling with anxiety symptoms and panic attacks. I was pretty discouraged and feeling even more out of control of my life. I remember saying to my therapist, "I don't understand why I'm not getting any better. I'm accepting my anxiety, and I'm saying all the right things. What am I doing wrong?" That's when I was told to make my recovery a lifetime goal. Now, that wasn't exactly what I wanted to hear. A lifetime meant forever, and I just wanted to be done with all this so that I could get on with my life.

My therapist also suggested that I say to myself, This is who I am today. I couldn't imagine how that could help in any way, but I found myself saying it many times over for a long time after that. It helped me accept where I was in my recovery at any given time.

It was still tempting to make six months a goal, but by the end of the first year of therapy, I accepted the fact that recovery would take as long as it would take. I came to realize that by giving myself a lifetime to get well, I was able to recover faster. Not putting a time limit on it took the pressure off. Looking back, I'm not even sure at what point my recovery actually took place. I just know that it was a long, slow process and that things are a whole lot better now.

⚜

A. Managing Our Anxiety: No Longer Anticipating Panic Attacks

During our process of recovery, we can reach a point where we no longer anticipate the occurrence of panic attacks. When we no longer care whether we panic, the attacks will eventually subside.

It is difficult to believe that we could ever have a receptive attitude toward something that affects our lives so dramatically as recurring panic attacks. However, with continued acceptance, repeated practice, and a supportive inner dialogue that allows us to experience the attacks, they tend to lose their uniqueness and eventually their power.

How can this be possible, we might ask, when we're unable to do something as simple as drive a car or shop for groceries without feeling as if we're going to faint, go crazy, or die? And how can telling ourselves that it's okay to be anxious possibly make a difference when we don't really feel that way? The fact is that even though permissive thoughts do not always bring about immediate success, with repeated practice they eventually help lower our level of concern. Very gradually, the more permissive we are of anxious feelings, the less attention we pay to them, not by denying them or distracting ourselves from them, but by allowing them to come to us and even trouble us.

Believability comes with repeated reassurance that our anxiety (even panic attacks) does not represent danger, and that we will be okay. We can remind ourselves that we've had many panic attacks before and have always survived. This will not be easy, because no matter how many panic attacks we've experienced in the past, the big what-if is always there to frighten us: Well, the last one was just a panic attack, but what if this time it's the real thing? We can't help wondering if our lives will continually be overshadowed by a fear of the next panic episode. Somewhere during the process of our recovery, however, we may reach a point where we are more receptive to the occurrence of panic attacks and therefore no longer devastated by them. It is then that they cease to be so troublesome to us and we find ourselves no longer concerned about whether or not we panic.

Before this happens, however, we've usually weathered any number of panic attacks with a 100 percent record of survival. We've gained an understanding of our body's reaction to stress and the physical symptoms of a panic episode. All of this has helped bring down our level of concern. With repeated practice of accepting and allowing the feelings, we emerge with confidence not only that we can survive the panic attacks, but that they are actually manageable. When we've reached the point where we're able to let go of the fear and no longer live in anticipation of the next panic attack, we know that we are well on our way to recovery.

It's as though we've gained a new perception of what is happening to us. The panic attacks are no longer a threat to our well-being, nor are they the focus of our lives. We no longer go through the day waiting for the next attack to occur; instead, we adopt the attitude that if it happens, it happens. We're able to get on with our life and take more risks with a minimum of avoidance. The more we let go of the fear, the less frequently the panic attacks occur, until they eventually subside.

B. Listening to Our Inner Dialogue: Nonpermissive/Permissive

The more permissive we are about panic attacks, the less troublesome they are. In the beginning, it is common to perceive our panic attacks as having catastrophic significance, even though they are essentially harmless. What causes problems for us is that we are troubled by them. We need to keep practicing the thought *It's all right to have panic attacks*. That takes the power out of them, and they gradually cease to bother us. When we are no longer troubled by them, it no longer matters to us whether or not we panic.

A-Talk: Nonpermissive	*B-Talk: Permissive*
1. This is probably only a panic attack, but then again, what if this time I'm really going to faint (or die or go crazy)?	1. I've had this feeling many times before. So what else is new? I'll try not to fight it and just let it happen!

A-Talk: *Nonpermissive*	B-Talk: *Permissive*
2. This is terrible! This is never going to go away! It's always going to be like this.	2. It's very possible that this will continue for some time. It will help if I can be accepting of that. But eventually it will change.
3. What if I keep having these panicky feelings?	3. The more I can allow them to happen, the better.
4. I hate this! I just can't keep letting this happen!	4. Fighting it is only going to make it worse. The best thing I can do is to just let it happen. If I panic, I panic!
5. Whatever is wrong with me must be very complex. They'll never be able to figure it out, and I'll have this forever.	5. What is wrong with me is complex, but not mysterious or hopeless. With time and patience, it will get better.

C. LIFESTYLE AWARENESS: ALLOWING MORE FLEXIBILITY IN OUR LIVES

We are aware that we have difficulty being flexible and that we tend to see things in all-or-nothing terms. It will help if we try to be less absolute in our thinking, allowing more flexibility in our lives.

Raising Our Level of Awareness

1. We do not easily allow flexibility, which often leads us to feeling stuck.	1. When confronted with problems, we will try to see that we have options and that we are free to make choices. Our unwillingness to do so leads us to feeling stuck.
2. We often think in terms of black or white without allowing for any gray areas; we see things as either right or wrong, or good or bad.	2. It will help if we become more aware of our rigid thinking and try to see the possibility of more gray areas in our lives.
3. We tend to impose rigid rules and standards on ourselves, allowing no deviations.	3. We will try to flow with life rather than be constantly constrained by rigid and/or self-imposed rules.

Raising Our Level of Awareness

4. We have a hard time being open to a less-than-perfect solution to a problem and therefore tend to give up.	4. Realizing that this is a result of our all-or-nothing thinking, we will try not to insist on always finding the perfect solution to a problem.

In the following testimonial, Delores talks about her early days of struggle with anxiety and panic attacks. She explains how she eventually was able to reach a point in her recovery where the panic attacks weren't so devastating and she no longer had to face each day in fear.

The early days of agoraphobia were confusing and terrifying. I remember holding onto my desk at work and asking, What is happening to me? That was the fall of 1965. It's a wonder I was even able to hold down a job. In the beginning I had no idea what was happening, nor did the medical profession have any answers. For months I struggled with the belief that I was either seriously ill or that I was hopelessly caught in the grips of a mental illness, which only terrified me more. My days and nights consisted of fighting the feelings that had become so overwhelming. I was constantly analyzing them, asking Why? and desperately trying to cling to some sense of sanity. There were times I thought I was dying. A therapist said, "No, you're not dying, but there will be times when you'll wish you were." I didn't believe him at the time, but the day would come when I would understand what he meant only too well.

Survival was the name of the game in those early days. I wouldn't give up trying to find a solution to my problem. What I did discover was by hit or miss, since no one could give me any answers. One thing I learned was that keeping busy helped. Unfortunately, it was like being on a treadmill; I was okay until it stopped. My life became a whirlwind of activity with the ever present fear of what would happen if I ever stopped to relax. I also discovered that by not being so impressed with the feelings I was able to keep some perspective. (This was the "grit-your-teeth-and-plow-through" period.) Most important, I discovered that when I no longer cared whether I had a panic attack or not, they occurred less often. As though it were yesterday, I remember remarking to my doctor, "I've decided that if I pass out on the street someone will help me. I just don't care anymore." It was a beginning. Later, I was told by my therapist, "It's when you stop caring that it goes away." And that it did!

Therapy was the final step in my recovery. I learned definite strategies to use when dealing with panic attacks. A complete change of attitude evolved, which helped give me back my zest for life. Fear was replaced by accepting and allowing. My expectations were lowered; even my whirlwind pace was challenged. Someone had finally helped me to get off the treadmill.

STRATEGY 13

A. MANAGING OUR ANXIETY: RECOGNIZING OUR INNER STRENGTH

Although we sometimes feel helpless, we might try to be receptive to the idea that each of us has inner strength to draw upon when necessary.

If we were asked to write down what we consider some of our more positive characteristics, chances are that inner strength would not be on our list. For whatever reason—be it our perfectionism or our all-or-nothing thinking—we pass judgment on ourselves and see our anxiety as defective. Our difficulties with panic and avoidance have only convinced us further that we lack inner strength.

What we fail to take into consideration is that we are dealing with an anxiety disorder and that we really can't compare ourselves to people who don't have this problem. For instance, we probably ask ourselves why it's so easy for others to travel by air, get into elevators, or drive on the expressway, when it's so painfully difficult for us. We seem to overlook the fact that an anxiety disorder is a real disorder that puts us at a definite disadvantage.

In many ways, our anxiety disorder has put us at the same disadvantage as someone with a physical disability. The difference is that we see their disability as valid. For example, we wouldn't think it unusual for a person with a physical handicap to sit in an aisle seat at the theater rather than in the middle of the row. Yet we are quick to question our decision to do so.

Perhaps that's the key: we don't accept our problem as valid. If we did, we wouldn't be so hard on ourselves. We wouldn't consider ourselves lacking in inner strength. We tend to forget the tremendous amount of courage it takes for us to face each new day. Running a simple errand, driving a car, or eating in a restaurant requires a great deal of strength on our part. People who are not phobic have no idea how much inner strength we actually have and how much we depend on it to accomplish any of these tasks. Unfortunately, neither do we. What a revelation it is when we discover that beneath all this fear is indeed a source of inner strength. It helps to remind ourselves that we are not the weaklings we sometimes perceive ourselves to be. Trying to be receptive to this idea will help give us more confidence to cope with difficult situations as we move forward in our recovery.

B. LISTENING TO OUR INNER DIALOGUE: NONACCEPTANCE/ACCEPTANCE

Those of us with anxiety disorders invariably suffer from low self-esteem. But the more we recover from our problem, the better we will feel about ourselves; and the better we feel about ourselves, the more we will recover. The more we accept our negative sense of self, the less troubled we will be by it and the more we will start liking ourselves. At that time the most difficult challenge will be to accept good feelings about ourselves.

A-Talk: Nonacceptance

1. I'm always going to have this! There's nothing I can do about it!

2. This is ridiculous! I should be able to do all the things that other people are able to do.

3. I should pull myself together and just do it!

4. I feel like such a coward.

B-Talk: Acceptance

1. I can try to accept that I might be dealing with this for a long time. The anxiety will become more manageable with patience and practice.

2. If I had a physical disability, I would not feel that I had to do the same as other people. The problem is that I'm not giving myself permission to have an anxiety problem.

3. I don't have to pull myself together. Actually, it would help if I allowed myself to have an anxiety problem.

4. It's okay to be afraid—it's all a part of having an anxiety disorder. Besides, it takes a great deal of courage to take the risks I'm taking.

A-Talk: Nonacceptance	*B-Talk: Acceptance*
5. I just don't seem to have what it takes to manage this.	5. For now, it helps to remind myself that I have the inner strength necessary to get through this one day at a time. With time and practice, my confidence in my ability to manage this will improve.

C. Lifestyle Awareness: Low Self-Esteem

We are aware that many of us are dealing with low self-esteem. We will try to be more accepting of good feelings about ourselves.

Raising Our Level of Awareness

1. Our self-esteem suffers because we believe that it comes from achieving. Unfortunately, we have a difficult time satisfying our high standards.	1. It will help if we try to be good to ourselves by setting up reasonable expectations.
2. Many of us have internalized an inner dialogue of self-deprecating statements concerning every aspect of our behavior; e.g., *I'm not good enough!* or *I'm not smart enough!*	2. We might introduce new ideas with a more nurturing inner dialogue so that there will be better balance between our A-talk and B-talk.
3. It is difficult for us to accept praise; we tend to discredit what we have done.	3. It will help if we try to be more accepting of good feelings about ourselves and our accomplishments, no matter how small they seem. When someone praises us, we will try saying thank you without explanation.
4. In our desire for approval, we sometimes say what we think the other person wants to hear rather than what we are really thinking.	4. Rather than discounting ourselves, we might boost our self-esteem if we risk voicing our own thoughts and opinions, even if they differ from someone else's.

5. Low self-esteem affects our ability to deal with everyday challenges and makes it difficult for us to make necessary changes in our lives.	5. It might help if we remind ourselves that our ability to cope with difficult tasks or make necessary changes will improve as our self-esteem improves.

We often see ourselves as lacking inner strength, while we see those around us as strong. At some point in our recovery, we begin to see ourselves in a different light and come to realize that we really do have a great deal of courage. Yvonne tapped into her inner strength when she took the risk of driving a long distance on the expressway.

Recently, I drove down Highway 18, something many people do every day. For me, however, it was quite an accomplishment, since it was the first time in eight years I had driven alone that far on the expressway. A year ago I wouldn't have made the trip because I didn't have the necessary tools to work with. But I have been part of a support group and have read informative books, both of which have helped prepare me to take such risks.

What also helped me that day was a burning desire to drive on the expressway. As I sat behind the wheel, I told myself, Getting to my destination is more important than how I'm feeling. My heart beat faster and my breathing was harder, but I just kept thinking, I really don't care! I just knew I was going to do it! Nothing could have stopped me that particular day. As I told myself, I don't care anymore, the anxiety diminished. Not caring really seemed to make a difference. As I got closer to my destination I got on a high—a natural high. I believe there's a power within you and you can do whatever you want.

STRATEGY 14

A. MANAGING OUR ANXIETY: REACHING OUT TO OTHERS

As we gain a better understanding of our anxiety problem and move ahead in our recovery, we can continue to benefit by reaching out to others who need support and encouragement.

We have learned that we are not alone, that our problem has a name, that others experience many of the same symptoms and are concerned about the problem of avoidance. We are aware of the importance of accepting, allowing, and taking risks. As we continue to learn a nurturing inner dialogue and helpful strategies in dealing with anxiety and panic attacks, our perception of what is happening to us is gradually changing. The more we learn about our anxiety problem, the less of a mystery it becomes. Perhaps we are even beginning to talk about our fear after having kept it a secret for so long.

Each of us experiences recovery in our own way. It might take longer for some of us than others. In the meantime it is important that we try not to compare ourselves with others who are going through the recovery process and that we try to be patient with our own progress. We know that setbacks are a necessary part of our recovery. There are times when we feel discouraged, but this is to be expected. It will help to remind ourselves that even if we're not there yet, we will eventually be able to see the light at the end of the tunnel. It is easy to fall back into old habits and shaming inner dialogue, but we can get back on track by continuing to see our therapist, attending a support group, and focusing on helpful strategies and supportive inner dialogue.

Those of us who have made progress in our own recovery often want to help those who are still struggling. Perhaps it is because we can relate to the feeling of isolation, the overwhelming fear of loss of control, and the sense of grief over that lost person we once knew. For whatever reason, *when we reach out to help others, we also help ourselves.*

We can help other anxiety and panic sufferers by sharing the strategies and inner dialogue that have helped us through difficult situations, and by giving them encouragement and support. In a group situation, we are able to see the progress we have made when new members share their experiences, and we will benefit from seeing that what has worked for us can work for others as well. Our simply being there reassures them that they are not alone.

Here are four effective ways of reaching out to others:

- Share positive experiences such as risk-taking, effective inner dialogue, and other helpful strategies. (To prevent adding to the other person's distress, avoid symptom-swapping and becoming preoccupied with the problem.)
- Share information about helpful books and articles on anxiety and phobias.
- Offer to go out together into public places to practice learned strategies.
- Organize a support group. (See Appendix.)

People suffering from anxiety and panic attacks are looking for answers, but more than that, they are reaching out for a sense of hope. Those of us who have made it through the rough times can give them that hope by sharing our experience and knowledge. Through our example, many will find comfort in knowing that recovery is possible.

B. LISTENING TO OUR INNER DIALOGUE: LIMITING/NONLIMITING

We might think that once we are recovered we will want to walk away from the past and just get on with our lives. In some cases this is true. We might be concerned that continuing to delve into anxiety problems will result in a setback. Or perhaps we might feel that we don't have anything important to offer anyone else. Many of us, however, feel that our experiences can be helpful to others and have found that there is much to be gained in continuing to give support and encouragement to those who are still suffering.

A-Talk: Limiting

1. I should be making more progress. Others seem further along in recovery than I am.

2. I'm not sure how I could be of any help to someone else dealing with this problem.

3. The risks I've taken are no big deal. They aren't important enough to share with others.

4. Now that I'm doing so well, it's probably better to forget what happened and just go on with my life.

5. What if I experience anxiety symptoms when discussing someone else's anxiety problem?

B-Talk: Nonlimiting

1. It would be better not to compare myself with others—we all move at our own pace. I can try to be patient with my own progress.

2. Perhaps sharing some of my own experiences would be helpful to others. I can talk about risks I've taken and helpful strategies I've used.

3. The risks I've taken and the strategies I've used are a big deal, and could be very helpful to others.

4. I certainly have that choice, as long as I'm not running away from the problem or pretending it never happened.

5. Discussing anxiety does not necessarily bring it about. If it does, I'll be able to deal with it. I've learned how to manage my anxiety. Besides, the benefits will outweigh any temporary discomfort I might experience.

C. Lifestyle Awareness: Being Actively Involved

We are aware that we feel better when we are actively involved, whether at we are working, helping others, or pursuing leisure-time activities.

Raising Our Level of Awareness

1. Many of us become so involved in our busy schedules that we seldom take time for ourselves. Then we feel guilty when we do so.

1. We will try to keep a healthy balance in our lives by allowing time for relaxation, leisure activities, or special interests.

2. Feeling depressed or fatigued, we tend to lose interest in fun or leisure activities.

2. Becoming involved, even getting excited about something, will actually help us refocus our energies into other channels.

3. For some of us, the anxiety and panic can become overwhelming so that we find it difficult to work outside the home.

3. We need to allow ourselves to take time off when necessary. However, working can be therapeutic. We might want to consider a part-time job, temporary work, or working in our home where we can set our own hours.

4. Because we feel needy ourselves, we sometimes find it difficult to focus on the needs of other people.

4. There are times when all we can do is take care of ourselves. But when we're ready, and if we so choose, it might help to become involved in a volunteer program that gives us the opportunity to help others. This can be both therapeutic and rewarding.

One of the advantages of being part of a support group is that people within the group have the opportunity to help one another. Bev tells us how she was able to get out and practice with another group member.

> My experience of sharing with a person I met in my support group has been very rewarding to me (as well as to her). We share survival techniques that work for us. We can depend on each other's honesty in difficult situations. We give feedback if it is asked for. Sometimes we just listen.
>
> Recently my friend returned from a trip to the West Coast, where she spent time with family and friends. On returning home she was depressed and experienced a lot of anxiety. The aftermath of leaving her "comfort zone" left her feeling helpless and hopeless. She was feeling out of control. We attended a support group meeting that evening. The discussion was on slowing down. What a perfect fit! We talked on the way home. She was glad to have found the warmth and comfort of friends. The days that followed were

difficult. But, as always, the feelings of panic and despair did pass.

So many times it has helped me to see myself in an earlier time of my recovery by listening and observing my friend's pain, knowing in my heart of hearts that recovery is a process and that I am continuing to get better and better. It is great to have found someone I can connect with and share feelings, risk-taking, and experiences with.

PART 3

INTEGRATION: TAKING RISKS

I can do just about everything now without all that anxiety. I hardly give it a thought anymore. What helped me the most . . . was to accept *it* and *allow it to happen. When I no longer cared if I had a panic attack, I quit having them.*

—LORI

PUTTING THE PROGRAM TO WORK

One of the first questions people reading this book might ask is, Can these cognitive strategies really help me? Many people have lost hope of ever getting well. They have simply given up, feeling there is no way out of their dilemma. But there is a way out, and the strategies discussed in this book can help. They worked for us, and they're now working for others.

The following pages list fourteen common places people experience anxiety or panic. For each place, the discussion is divided into two parts: anticipatory anxiety and the actual event. Each part gives examples of two types of self-talk: the "What-Ifs" (A-talk) and the "So-Be-Its" (B-talk). There is also a list of helpful strategies that you may want to try. They are not necessarily related to the specific examples listed in the "What-Ifs" and "So-Be-Its" columns; rather, they are general suggestions that you can use in that situation.

As you read through the situations, you will find that much of the self-talk is the same—which is precisely the point. There are only so many ways to ask, "What if I have a panic attack?" and only so many ways to say, "Go ahead and panic!" The answers do vary, but they all mean the same thing: try to stay with the feelings and allow the panic to run its course. These are examples of inner dialogue, much of which you will be able to relate to. More than likely, you have your own self-talk to add to the list.

What we say to ourselves can make a difference in how we deal with anxiety or panic in any given situation. As stated previously, those of us with anxiety problems tend to be very good at A-talk (which is shaming and nonpermissive). Since this kind of self-talk is highly internalized—automatic, chronic, and situated in the subconscious—it is difficult to simply replace it with another kind of self-talk, namely, B-talk (which is nurturing and allowing). But that is not what we are suggesting. Rather than try to replace our A-talk, we can challenge it with B-talk and create a balance between the two.

Since this part of the book is meant to be used for reference, there is a lot of repetition. As we see certain strategies and inner dialogue repeated for each of the places listed in the following pages, we become more and more aware of their importance in almost any given situation.

The most common helpful strategies include the following:

1. *Seeing each situation as an opportunity to practice.* We can allow the anxiety to be there rather trying to perform anxiety-free.
2. *Keeping our expectations low.* If we approach a feared situation with low expectations, allowing for any discomfort, we limit the possibility of failure.
3. *Giving ourselves permission to leave at any time.* Staying in a situation gives us practice in going with the feelings; leaving gives us practice working with the self-shaming thoughts that might occur as a result of our decision. We benefit either way.
4. *Visualizing the worst that can happen and what we might do to get through it.* Visualizing the worst is a pretty scary thought. But it gives us practice in going through a situation and mentally generating helpful strategies for dealing with our anxiety—before it actually occurs.
5. *Trying to be receptive to coping well.* Seeing ourselves as coping well might be difficult for some of us because we can't believe that anything can turn out well.

An important part of recovery is sharing with others the risks we have taken and the helpful strategies that have made them possible. Some of these risks are recorded in the following pages. These testimonials show us how other people deal with their anxiety, catastrophic thoughts, and panic attacks. Words such as *accept* and *allow*, and phrases such as *going with the feeling* are used repeatedly. The testimonials do not delve into the problem itself but focus on strategies individuals have used to get through difficult situations. What we want to know is, *Now that I have the problem, where do I go from here?*

It is hoped that these stories of courage will be an inspiration and a reassurance that *our anxiety and panic attacks can become manageable.* Knowing that many others are facing the same challenges we are may help take away our feeling of isolation. With acceptance, understanding, and supportive self-talk, we too can gain confidence to practice taking necessary risks. Many of us have reached the other side of anxiety and panic by facing it and going through it.

GOING TO CHURCH

Being in church can be a problem for many of us who are phobic, because we feel we can't get up and leave when we want to. We think that we will be very conspicuous and that people will wonder why we are leaving. It will help if we give ourselves options, such as choosing where to sit or where to go in case of a panic attack.

Anticipatory Anxiety

The What-Ifs	The So-Be-Its	Other Helpful Strategies
What if I can't get out to church on Sunday?	I could give myself the option of not going and then practice being okay with that decision.	*I could see my decision to attend church as something I want to do, not as something I have to do. I might also remind myself of the meaning it has for me.*
What if I get there and panic?	The best thing I could do is to allow that to happen.	
What if my family wants to sit up front?	I could either sit up front with them or choose to sit toward the back. Either way would be good practice.	*I could try to slow down and give myself plenty of time to get ready for church.*
		I could try to keep my expectations low about how well I'll do.

At Church

The What-Ifs	The So-Be-Its	Other Helpful Strategies
What if I panic?	Go ahead and panic. It's only a feeling and I'm not in any danger.	*I can have a place in mind where I might go (e.g., the foyer) and then practice an inner dialogue that supports that decision.*
What if I have to leave?	It's okay to leave. It will help if I give myself permission to do so.	

The What-Ifs	The So-Be-Its	Other Helpful Strategies
What will people think?	Chances are, people really aren't going to be concerned about why I'm leaving.	*I will try to be willing to ask for help if necessary.*
What if I faint and make a fool of myself?	I'm only having a thought about fainting. Most likely that won't happen. Even if it did, fainting is not foolish.	*If I feel that I have to leave during the service, I'll try to escape slowly.* *I can give myself permission to sit in back of the church and/or in an aisle seat.* *I will practice allowing the anxiety to be there rather than trying so hard to fix it.*

I had my first panic attack in church. From then on I would come up with any number of excuses for not going. When I did manage to get there, I wanted to sit as far back in the church as possible. However, I usually ended up sitting toward the front with my family, white-knuckling it through the entire service. I was really scared! I just knew I was going to pass out right there in front of everyone. I fought hard to stay in control as the anxiety got worse. I just wanted to get out of there. I tried to distract myself by focusing on objects around me—anything—just so I wouldn't think about how I was feeling.

It wasn't until I found out that I had a panic disorder and learned how to handle my anxiety and panic attacks that things began to change. I'm not fighting the panic anymore, nor am I trying to distract myself. I know I can leave if I want to. Now I give myself options about where I want to sit, even if it means being away from my family. By doing this, I'm actually finding it easier to sit with them. I'm able to become involved in the service itself rather than being preoccupied with my anxiety. I no longer have to come up with excuses to stay home on Sunday (although I still give myself that option).

—KATE

97

GOING TO THE DENTIST

Another situation that can give us a trapped feeling is sitting in the dentist's chair. We might find that giving ourselves permission to get up out of the chair and move around can help to alleviate some of our anxiety. Having an understanding dentist is also helpful.

Anticipatory Anxiety

The What-Ifs	The So-Be-Its	Other Helpful Strategies
What if I can't go and have to cancel my appointment?	I will try to be okay with calling to say I can't make it. After all, I would cancel if I were physically ill and not question my doing so.	*I could try to set up an appointment at the last minute so I won't have to wait so long. That way there would be less anticipatory anxiety.*
How will I explain that I can't make it in?	I could explain my situation or just say that I'm not feeling well. I also have the option of not giving an explanation.	*I'll try not to have all the work done at once, but schedule multiple appointments.*
What if the dentist doesn't understand my problem and gets impatient with me?	If that happens, I'll manage the best I can and then find another dentist who is more understanding.	*It will help if I visit dentists in advance, explain my situation, and be sure they're empathetic.*
		It will help if I keep my expectations low about how well I'll do.

At the Dentist

The What-Ifs	The So-Be-Its	Other Helpful Strategies
What if I panic while I'm in the dentist chair?	I will try to allow that to happen and reassure myself that I'm not in any danger. If necessary, I'll simply get out of the chair.	*I can tell my dentist that I have a panic disorder and explain my situation.*

The What-Ifs	*The So-Be-Its*	*Other Helpful Strategies*
What if I make a fool of myself? What will the people in the office think?	My real concern is how I *feel* about what they might think. However, I'll try to feel okay about myself regardless of what they might be thinking.	*My dentist and I can work out a signal so he or she will know if I have to get out of the chair.*
What if I have to leave before the dentist is finished?	That probably won't happen, but if it does I'll just have to leave.	*I can give myself a way out so that I won't feel trapped. (Giving myself a way out doesn't mean that I have to take it.)*

It has been a real risk for me, but I'm finally getting back for my dental appointments. For a long time I dreaded going to the dentist, even for a checkup. It got to the point where I just stopped going altogether. Now that I'm back, I'm trying to do some new things I've learned. Instead of trying so hard to control my anxiety, I'm allowing myself to feel anxious, even panicky, while I'm at the dentist's office. The problem is being in that chair. It's not like I can just get up and leave when I want to. Well, I guess I can. At least that's what I'm working on now—telling myself that I can get up out of the dentist's chair if I'm feeling anxious. So far this seems to be helping. Something else that has made a difference is that I decided to tell the dentist about my anxiety problem. He has been pretty understanding and has even encouraged me to get up and move around if necessary. Just knowing that he's aware, as well as understanding, has been a big help.

—GEORGE

99

GOING TO THE SUPERMARKET

Something as routine as going to the store to buy groceries can be very difficult for us. Long, narrow aisles and inconvenient access to the door add to our concern. The checkout line can be especially difficult because we feel trapped. We fear that once we're in line, leaving our grocery cart behind and heading out the door would be conspicuous.

Anticipatory Anxiety

The What-Ifs	*The So-Be-Its*	*Other Helpful Strategies*
What if I can't get out to do my grocery shopping?	I could wait and do it later, or ask someone to do it with me (or for me).	*I could start practicing by going to a store close by, one that I'm familiar with.*
What if I panic on the way?	I'll try to just let it happen. It's only a feeling. I won't be in any danger.	*I'll allow myself to visualize the worst that can happen and what I might do to get through it. Or I can try to be receptive to the idea of coping well.*
What if I have to wait in line?	I could go at a time when it isn't busy.	
What if my hand shakes while I'm writing a check?	I could write part of the check before I get there. I could also use cash.	*It will help if I keep my expectations low about how well I'll do.*

At the Grocery Store

The What-Ifs	*The So-Be-Its*	*Other Helpful Strategies*
What if I faint?	I'm only dealing with a thought about fainting. Chances are that won't happen.	*While shopping I will try to slow down!* *I can keep my list short and buy a few items at a time.*

The What-Ifs	*The So-Be-Its*	*Other Helpful Strategies*
What if I get to the back of the store and I can't leave?	My legs will carry me to the door, even if it doesn't feel that way.	*I can practice allowing myself to be anxious.*
I'm really feeling strange. What if this time it isn't anxiety?	It *is* only anxiety. I'm not in any danger. It will help if I just try to go with the feeling.	
What if I panic and have to leave my cart?	It really is okay to walk away from the cart and leave the store.	

Well, it happened just like I thought it would. I had a panic attack at the grocery store right at the checkout line. I could feel it coming. My heart started beating fast and my legs were wobbly, even though I knew I could walk. The cashier didn't know what to do. She kept asking me if I'd like to sit down and have a glass of water. She asked me if I'd be all right, and of course I said yes. The only excuse I could think of to tell her was that I was dieting. Rather than leaving the store immediately, I chose to stay. In the back of my mind I knew I could make it. I tried not to attach any danger to the feelings. I managed to bag my groceries without any problems, even though my two-year-old was running off to the gum ball machine. I sure was glad to get outside after that one. In spite of that experience I managed to go back to the store on another occasion. This time I was alone. I knew that I could have another anxiety attack, but I also knew that facing the fear would help me get through this. Keeping my expectations low and giving myself the option of not buying everything on my grocery list, I made it through my shopping without any feelings of panic.

—KATHY

Going to the Hair Salon

Making appointments of any kind is difficult for those of us who suffer from panic attacks. Calling ahead for a haircut is no exception. The anticipatory anxiety is usually worse than the actual event. Once we're there, we manage to draw on whatever strategies we have to deal with the discomfort.

Anticipatory Anxiety

The What-Ifs	The So-Be-Its	Other Helpful Strategies
What if I'm feeling terrible that day and just can't get out?	I have the option of not going. If I feel I can't get out, I will at least have the opportunity to practice being okay with that decision.	*It will help if I don't make my appointment too far in advance.*
What if they get mad at me for canceling at the last minute?	That just might be the consequence of my decision, but I don't have to worry about it now. When the time comes I'll handle it the best way I can.	*I'll try to make my appointment for a time when the salon is less likely to be busy.* *I'll give myself permission to ask someone to go with me.*
What if I get there (or halfway there) and panic?	It will help if I can allow that to happen. I can always turn around and go home.	*It will help if I keep my expectations low about how well I'll do.*

At the Hair Salon

The What-Ifs	The So-Be-Its	Other Helpful Strategies
What if I panic halfway through the haircut?	It's okay to leave. Trying to see some humor in it might help.	*I can tell the hair stylist that I'm worried about panicking.*

The What-Ifs	*The So-Be-Its*	*Other Helpful Strategies*
What if other people notice? What will they think?	My real concern is how I *feel* about what others might think. I'll try to feel okay about myself regardless of what they might be thinking.	*I'll try to give myself permission to get up and move around if necessary.* *I can plan my escape.*
What if I explain my situation and the hair stylist is ill at ease?	That's the stylist's problem and he or she will have to deal with it.	

The beauty parlor is another place where I have a problem. First of all, I don't like making the appointment and then wondering whether or not I'm going to be able to get there. The last time I went to get my hair cut I was fortunate to get in the same day, which meant I didn't have that much time to think about it. Once I was there, I did pretty well. I used some of the strategies that we had been talking about in my support group. I think I surprised myself when I found out that they actually did work. I used to get two-thirds through a haircut and then think, What if I panic and have to get out of here? *I'd imagine myself running down the street with my hair two different lengths, looking like an idiot. This time when I had those thoughts, I told myself to go ahead and panic, that nothing more would happen and that the chances of my running down the street were pretty slim, since it was only a thought. Actually, I opted for the bathroom as my getaway place, if I needed one. It seemed to help. I actually laughed when I thought about running out of the shop, which helped relieve some of my anxiety.*

I wound up telling the beautician that I sometimes feel anxious and that it helps if I can get up and walk around. She seemed perfectly okay with this, which helped a lot. So I no longer had to hide my anxiety. I'm finding that the more accepting I am of my situation, and the more options I give myself, the better.

—KAREN

103

SHOPPING AT THE MALL

We are sometimes reluctant to venture out on our own and find it necessary to rely on a support person. This can eventually create a problem for us, since we often want to do things on our own. With time and practice we can become independent again and enjoy shopping alone.

Anticipatory Anxiety

The What-Ifs	*The So-Be-Its*	*Other Helpful Strategies*
What if I just can't make it out that day?	I could always change my mind. I don't have to go.	*At first I could choose a mall close to home, one that I'm familiar with.*
What if I panic on the way?	I'll try to allow it to happen. It's only a feeling and I won't be in any physical danger.	*I'll allow myself to visualize the worst that can happen and what I might do to get through it.*
What if I get there and I can't make it back?	I could always ask for help or muddle through the best I can.	*I'll give myself permission to ask someone to go with me.*
What if I faint?	That's only a thought about fainting. Chances are, that's not going to happen. If it does, however, someone will help me.	*It will help if I keep my expectations low about how well I'll do.*

At the Mall

The What-Ifs	*The So-Be-Its*	*Other Helpful Strategies*
What if I panic?	I'll just go ahead and panic. I won't be in any physical danger.	*I can choose a time when the mall is not too busy.*
		I'll try to slow down and not rush.
		At first, I can shop with someone and practice short periods of separation.

The What-Ifs	The So-Be-Its	Other Helpful Strategies
What if I make a fool of myself?	That's only a thought that I'm having. It's never happened before, and it probably won't happen now.	*It might help to pick out a sales clerk as my "safe person" to go to for help if necessary. Chances are it won't be.*
Now that I'm here, what if I can't get out?	My legs will carry me to the door, even if it doesn't seem that way now.	*I could begin by giving myself permission to use the outside door of each store, whenever possible, rather than going through the mall.*
What if I have to leave?	There's nothing wrong with leaving as long as I'm okay with that decision.	

For a long time I couldn't go into a store without having an anxiety attack. I always found excuses so I wouldn't have to go shopping alone. During the past six months, while shopping with a support person, I've taken the opportunity to go off by myself for short periods in order to practice being on my own. Although I've been aware that I'm sometimes isolated from my partner, I've lowered my expectations and so allowed for some discomfort. I've discovered that I can do very well and have experienced little or no panic. After several practice sessions of this sort, I've been able to walk to different parts of the store alone. On one occasion, I actually went up to the second floor by myself, which had been impossible for me to do for a long time. Again, I experienced none of the familiar symptoms. Recently, my husband drove me to another large department store. I told him to just drop me off, that I would go in to get what I needed. "Are you sure?" he asked, somewhat surprised. I assured him that I would be fine. I knew that I could do it. I decided to buy just one item. That way, it wouldn't take very long. It worked! Again, all went well. I came out of the store knowing that I could do it. I really felt good about myself for having accomplished this.

—EMILY

❧

105

GOING TO A RESTAURANT

Going out for lunch with a friend is something that almost every-one has the opportunity to do. Right? Well, for those of us with panic disorder, it just isn't that easy. When we do reach a point in our recovery where we can venture into a restaurant, we view our new success with disbelief. This is especially true if we have experi-enced panic attacks over a long period of time.

Anticipatory Anxiety

The What-Ifs	The So-Be-Its	Other Helpful Strategies
What if I'm having a bad day? I'll be uncomfort-able all the while I'm there.	I'll try to allow myself to be uncomfortable. That's the worst that will happen.	*I'll allow myself to visual-ize the worst that might happen and what I might do to get through it.*
What if I decide I just can't go?	It's okay to back out. I'll practice being okay with that decision.	*I could try to be recep-tive to images of coping well.*
What if my friends notice? What will they think?	My real concern is how I feel about what they might think. However, I'll try to feel okay about myself regardless of what they might think.	*I could start by going to a restaurant close to home, one that I'm familiar with.*
		I'll try to keep my expec-tations low about how well I'll do.

At the Restaurant

The What-Ifs	The So-Be-Its	Other Helpful Strategies
What if I have a panic attack?	It's just a panic attack. I'll go ahead and have it. I won't be in any physi-cal danger.	*I can give myself permis-sion to sit at a table close to the door.*

The What-Ifs	The So-Be-Its	Other Helpful Strategies
What if I make a fool of myself?	I'm only having a thought about making a fool of myself. Chances are that won't happen.	*I can practice allowing the anxiety to be there rather than trying so hard to fix it.*
What if I have to get out of here?	It's okay to leave. It will give me an opportunity to practice being okay with that.	*I'll give myself a way out so that I won't feel trapped. (Giving myself a way out doesn't mean I have to take it.)*
What if I've already ordered?	I can always say that I'm not feeling well. I really can leave if I have to.	

I can hardly believe that I've been going to so many restaurants lately for lunch, dinner, and so on. Going to a restaurant was always uncomfortable for me. Now I'm finding it a lot easier. I'm sure this has to do with just going out and doing it. Recently I had to wait for a half hour in the crowded entryway of a restaurant before we could get a table. After the long wait, we were finally seated way in back of the room. In spite of this, I did fine! Throughout the situation I just gave myself permission to leave at any time.

Although I still feel a little uneasy before going into a restaurant, I find that I'm comfortable once I'm actually there. I figure that once I'm at my table, I'll just sit back and go with the feeling if necessary. Practicing, taking risks, and getting involved have really made a big difference for me.

—MARION

Going to the Theater, Concerts, or Large Group Events

In retrospect, we might find some of our experiences amusing, even though they were terrifying at the time. It certainly is to our advantage to have coping skills to rely on. However, when all else fails, muddling can sometimes get us through a difficult situation.

Anticipatory Anxiety

The What-Ifs	The So-Be-Its	Other Helpful Strategies
What if I'm feeling sensitized that day? I'll have a miserable time.	It will be good practice. The worst that could happen is that I'll feel miserable.	*I'll allow myself to visualize the worst that might happen and what I might do to get through it. Or I can try to be receptive to images of coping well.*
If I make a commitment, I'll only be anxious thinking about it.	I'll deal with the anxiety the best I can. Besides, I could always change my mind. It's no big deal.	
If at the last minute I can't go, I'll disappoint my family or friends.	They could still go. Someone else could use my ticket.	*If I order tickets in advance I could arrange to sit in an aisle seat or near the back of the theater.*
		I could familiarize myself with the theater and its location in advance.
		I could give myself plenty of time to get ready and not wait until the last minute.

108

At the Event

The What-Ifs	*The So-Be-Its*	*Other Helpful Strategies*
What if I panic and make a fool of myself?	I'll just go ahead and panic. It's only a feeling and I'm not in any physical danger. I'm only having a thought about making a fool of myself. That's never happened before and it probably won't happen now. However, the more permissive I am of having a panic attack, the better.	*I'll try to stay with my feelings rather than avoid them, and practice allowing the anxiety to be there.* *I can stay on the outside corridor rather than mix with the crowd.* *I'll keep my expectations low about how well I'll do.*
What if I faint?	Chances are I won't faint. I'm only having a thought about fainting. Besides, if I did, someone would help me.	
What if I can't get out of here?	I can sit in an aisle seat toward the back and have access to a door.	
What if I have to leave?	It's okay to leave. It will help if I give myself permission to do so. I can practice being okay with that decision.	
What if I get separated from my family or friends?	We can plan where to meet if we get separated. I can also have my friend paged or even find my way home by myself.	

Recently, I had an experience at the theater that was so frightening it required every strategy I could come up with in order to get through it. We went to see The Little Match Girl. *Once there, I planned my escape route just in case. We were in the balcony in the center of a single row, so the quickest way out was to climb over the back of the seat. Once I realized that I had limited access to escape, I began to experience a wave of anxiety. So I sat back and focused on accepting and floating. The curtain was about to go up, and the lights were lowered. No, not lowered—extinguished. That did it. In the total darkness, I frantically searched for the exit sign to the right of the stage in order to alleviate the claustrophobia. The sign wasn't on. All my focus on accepting and floating vanished.*

It seemed an eternity before a small flicker of light appeared on the stage. Behind me I could see a faint outline of the back of the seat. I told my family I was leaving, climbed over the seat, and felt my way through the darkness toward the door. The flickering light from the stage did little to help me find my way. Engulfed by the darkness, I was now separated from my family and totally disoriented. I was terrified! I concentrated on escaping slowly and telling myself, It's only a perception—go ahead and have it! *As the symptoms persisted, I reminded myself that this was what phobias were all about and that it was perfectly okay for me to leave.*

When I finally made it to the door, I explained my plight to the usher. He took me downstairs, where I continued to watch the play from the back of the theater. Toward the end of the performance, the lights went out again, but this time I chose to stay. I knew I had easy access to the door and could reach it quickly if I had to, since I was sitting on the aisle seat. With this in mind, I allowed the intense darkness to penetrate and focused on all of the feelings that accompanied it. I felt good about how I had handled the situation, and was glad to have had the necessary skills to get me through it. In retrospect, I find the entire episode slightly amusing.

—JANE

❧

GOING TO A SOCIAL EVENT OR PARTY

We miss out on many enjoyable social events because we avoid places where we have experienced intense anxiety or panic. The problem becomes even more complex when we plan to attend these functions with other people, since we're afraid we will spoil their fun if we decide we can't go or if we have to leave because of our anxiety.

Anticipatory Anxiety

The What-Ifs	The So-Be-Its	Other Helpful Strategies
What if I feel awful that night and can't go?	I could always call and explain that I'm not feeling well.	*I'll try to allow myself to visualize the worst that can happen and what I might do to get through it. Or I can try to be receptive to images of coping well.*
If I can't go I'll be letting down my friend. I'll really feel guilty if I spoil someone else's fun.	I probably will feel guilty if it's my fault. But would I feel guilty if I couldn't go because I had a severe headache?	
What if I'm so preoccupied with the way I feel that I won't have a good time?	Even if I don't have a good time, it will be good practice for me to be there.	*I could give myself the option of dealing with it at the time.* *I could try to keep my expectations low about how well I'll do.*
What if I make a fool of myself?	I haven't made a fool of myself before and probably won't now.	

At the Social Event or Party

The What-Ifs	The So-Be-Its	Other Helpful Strategies
What if I have to leave? How would I explain it to my friends?	It's okay to leave. I can always say that I'm not feeling well.	*I'll try to have a place in mind where I can go if I feel the need to escape, such as a room away from the crowd.*

111

The What-Ifs	The So-Be-Its	Other Helpful Strategies
What if I panic while talking to one of the other guests?	I'll try to allow the panic the best I can or excuse myself and leave the room.	*It will help if the person I'm with knows my concern and is supportive of any decision I make, even if it means leaving.*
What if people notice? What will they think?	People usually can't tell when I'm panicking. But if they do notice, I'll try to be okay with that.	*It will help if I practice allowing the anxiety to be there.*

February 2 marked a big social event at the Art Institute. In spite of my fear of crowds, I didn't want to miss it. As my husband and I waited for the doors to open, the lobby filled up to the point where it was definitely interfering with my comfort level. I glanced around at some possible escape routes just in case I had to leave. When the doors opened, I felt the crowd move forward. There was a time when I would have looked away from the crowd or tried hard to concentrate on something else, just to distract myself. Instead, I chose to stay in touch with what was happening. I was aware of the crowd and my feeling of being completely surrounded. Staying with the feelings and trying not to attach any danger to them, I soon found myself inside the museum and involved in the evening's activities.

But the biggest challenge of the evening was yet to come. When we left the auditorium, I realized that the room we were entering had become densely crowded. I felt a wave of panic as I looked around for an alternate route. There was no other way out. I *really felt trapped! I sensed a need to rush ahead, but instead I concentrated on slowing down. Staying with my fear, I decided I'd manage the best I could, even if it meant muddling through. It was wall-to-wall people. I felt my legs go weak. Turning to my husband I said, "I don't think I can go into that crowd! "Follow me!" he said, and I held on to his suit coat while he cleared a path through the room. The thought of staying alone kept me moving, weak knees and all!* I don't believe I'm doing this! *I thought.*

We had one more room to go through, and it was just as crowded as the one we had left. Again I looked for an alternate route, and this time I found one. I went through the Ancient Gallery and bypassed the crowds, reaching the front entrance in much less time.

I felt okay about opting for the easy way out. I had nothing to prove to myself or anyone else. At one time I would have asked myself, What is happening to me? What is wrong? But now I know the answers. Finding ways to deal with my phobia has become a way of life that I'm accepting. Had it not been for this acceptance and an understanding of my anxiety problem, I would have missed the excitement of the evening.

—JOAN

GOING TO WORK, TO A CONFERENCE, OR ON A JOB INTERVIEW

At one time or another, we all experience stress in the workplace. This creates a problem for us, because we're afraid that we'll panic in front of our co-workers. This is especially true during a job interview. Whether we are the person being interviewed or the one who is doing the interviewing, we put ourselves in a situation where we feel trapped.

Anticipatory Anxiety

The What-Ifs	The So-Be-Its	Other Helpful Strategies
What if I panic?	It will help if I just let it happen. I'm not in any physical danger.	*I'll allow myself to visualize the worst that might happen and work my way through it.*
What if I'm in a situation where I can't leave?	I really could leave *any* situation if I have to. I could always make up an excuse. (I would leave if I were physically ill.) Leaving may have consequences, but I *could* do it.	*I could also visualize the way I want it to be and try to see myself doing it.* *I could give myself the option of dealing with it at the time.*
What if I make a fool of myself? What will they think?	I'm only having a thought about making a fool of myself. Chances are, that won't happen.	

At Work, at a Conference, or on a Job Interview

The What-Ifs	The So-Be-Its	Other Helpful Strategies
What if I panic?	It's all right to panic. I won't be in any physical danger.	*I will try to allow all feelings, staying with them as much as possible.*

The What-Ifs	*The So-Be-Its*	*Other Helpful Strategies*
What if someone notices my anxiety?	Chances are no one will notice. But if someone does, I'll try to be okay with that. It might help to remind myself that most people are nervous during an interview.	*It will help if I try to slow down!* *I'll try to keep my expectations low about how well I'll do.*
How can I possibly leave?	I probably won't want to leave, but it is important that I give myself permission to do so; otherwise, I'll feel trapped. (Giving myself permission does not mean that I'll necessarily do it.)	
What if I lose my job because of my anxiety or panic attacks?	Chances are I won't. But if I do, so be it! This is only a thought about losing my job. It's okay to have it.	

The past few weeks I have been interviewing people for jobs. This has been a really good experience for me and a good chance for me to practice the various strategies I've learned. These are the techniques I used:

- *I allowed myself to feel anxious about interviewing people. I told myself my anxiety was normal and it was okay to have it.*
- *I told myself that I was going to feel anxious, but I was going to do it anyway.*
- *I told myself that the other person would likely be more nervous than I would be.*
- *I gave myself the option of having someone else do the interviewing if I didn't feel up to it.*

It was not the most pleasant experience for me, but the important thing is that I did it with the anxiety. (In the past I would not have done it at all.) This is progress! I did hire one person, and I am now allowing myself to feel the anxiety of having a new person around!

—DEBORAH

DRIVING ALONE

It helps to extend our boundaries gradually, taking it one step at a time. Our self-talk can make a big difference in how well we do when venturing out on our own, but there are also ways to make our practice sessions fun and adventuresome.

Anticipatory Anxiety

The What-Ifs	The So-Be-Its	Other Helpful Strategies
What if I'm too panicky to get out of the driveway?	Then I'll pull back into the garage and try to be okay with that.	*I will try to see my practice session as something I want to do, not something I have to do.*
What if I have a panic attack and there's no one there to help me?	The worst that will happen is that I'll panic. I'll muddle through the best I can. I can always turn around and come home.	*I can choose a time when there's very little traffic.*
What if I get lost?	If I feel lost, I'll do the best I can to take care of myself. I can always call for help.	*I'll try to keep my expectations low as to how well I'll do.*
		I can try to think of it as practice in allowing the anxiety to be there.

While Driving

The What-Ifs	The So-Be-Its	Other Helpful Strategies
What if I panic and cause an accident?	I will have time to pull over, and its okay to do that. My causing an accident is a thought, not a fact.	*At first, I can practice driving with someone. I can begin by having a friend sit in the front seat. Later, he or she can sit in back.*

The What-Ifs	The So-Be-Its	Other Helpful Strategies
What if the car breaks down and I'm stranded?	I'll manage the best I can, even if I have to muddle through. I can always call for help.	*I can drive alone in a familiar area close to home. I can start out by having someone follow me in another car.*
What if I panic and there's no one there to help?	I'll try to go with the feeling. I can get help if necessary. It might help to remind myself that what I'm really experiencing is a fear of isolation.	*I can take gradual risks with unfamiliar locations. Again, I might want to start with someone following me.*
		I can remind myself that my safety is within me and not in any given place.

I have been keeping track of my driving progress. I mark every street or area I drive by coloring it red on my map. I recently found myself looking at my map and felt I was becoming stagnant. I guess I hadn't been feeling like pushing myself (which is okay). But now I felt like extending my boundaries a little further. I decided to choose somewhere interesting or fun, just beyond the edge of my "red" zone. I made a list that included shopping malls, golf courses, friends' houses, etc. I'm now working on my list slowly and rewarding myself with a treat when I reach each desti-nation. When practicing, I allow myself to turn around at any time and try again another day. The process may take time, but I'll make time for each adventure.

—JANET

RIDING ON A BUS, IN A VAN, OR IN A CARPOOL

Sitting in the back of a bus, van, or car, where we do not have immediate access to a door, can make us feel trapped. It's certainly a situation where we need options. Our main concern is losing control and drawing attention to ourselves.

Anticipatory Anxiety

The What-Ifs	*The So-Be-Its*	*Other Helpful Strategies*
What if I just can't get into the vehicle?	I'll give myself the option of going back home and try to be okay with that decision.	*I will allow myself to visualize the worst that might happen and what I could do to get through it. Or I can try to be receptive to images of coping well.*
What if I lose control and make a fool of myself?	I'm only having a thought about losing control. Chances are it won't happen.	
What if I take a bus and get lost?	I can always ask for help, call a cab, or call a friend to come and get me.	*If I'm in a carpool, it might help if one other person riding in the car knows about my problem.*
What if I panic and I can't get off the bus?	My legs will carry me to the door, even though it doesn't seem that way now.	*I'll try to keep my expectations low about how well I'll do.*

On the Bus, in the Van, or in the Carpool

The What-Ifs	*The So-Be-Its*	*Other Helpful Strategies*
What if I panic?	I'll just go ahead and panic. It's only a feeling, and I'm not in any physical danger.	*I can practice riding a short distance with a friend, taking one block at a time. Later I can have my friend follow me in his or her car.*

119

The What-Ifs	The So-Be-Its	Other Helpful Strategies
What if people notice?	Chances are they won't be able to tell I'm having a panic attack. If they can, I'll just try to accept that.	*I can practice riding alone and give myself permission to get off, but have an alternate plan (such as calling a friend or a cab).*
What if I have to get off and I'm stranded?	I can always ask for help. I can also call a cab or call a friend to come and get me.	*I will try to be okay with asking for help.*
What if I get on the bus and can't find a seat near the door?	I'll just stand near the door.	*I will practice allowing the anxiety to be there.*

I really have a tough time when I'm out with friends or co-workers who are unaware of my anxiety problem, especially if I'm riding in someone else's car. I just don't feel in control of the situation. It sure can put a damper on an otherwise fun evening. Just recently, I went out on the town with some friends and ended up sitting in the back of a van. Talk about claustrophobic! My mind went into full gear. I wasn't sure how I was going to handle this one. But I knew I had to come up with something fast. I figured I could ask the person in front of me to exchange places (explaining that the back seat made me feel claustrophobic) or I could stay put and try to let the feeling run its course. I decided to stay with the uncomfortable feeling for a while and then, if necessary, ask the person in front of me to trade places. By just giving myself a way out I didn't feel so trapped. It turned out to be a fun evening after all.

—PAUL

DRIVING ON THE EXPRESSWAY

Driving on the expressway can give us a trapped feeling because of the fast-moving traffic and the distance between exits. We believe that if we panic we won't be able to pull over or get help when we need it.

Anticipatory Anxiety

The What-Ifs	*The So-Be-Its*	*Other Helpful Strategies*
What if the car breaks down on the expressway?	I could always seek help. It would be a good idea to take money with me in case I have to call a cab or a friend.	*I'll allow myself to visualize the worst that could happen and see myself dealing with it. Or I could try to be receptive to images of coping well.*
What if I get lost?	I'll probably feel lost, but I'll do the best I can to take care of myself. I could stop and ask for directions.	*I could give myself permission to take an alternate route, such as a frontage road or another back road. I really do have this option.*
What if I panic and there's no one around to help me?	The best thing I can do is to allow that to happen. I won't be in any danger. I can seek help if I feel there's a need for it.	*I'll try to keep my expectations low about how well I'll do.*

On the Expressway

The What-Ifs	*The So-Be-Its*	*Other Helpful Strategies*
What if I feel panicky while I'm out on the expressway?	I can get off at the next exit and take an alternate route. It will help if I try to be okay with that.	*I can begin practicing with a support person.* *I can give myself permission to drive in the far-right lane.*

121

The What-Ifs	*The So-Be-Its*	*Other Helpful Strategies*
What if I panic and cause an accident?	If I panic, I'll still have time to pull over. It really is okay to do that. Besides, that's only a thought about having an accident, not an actual event.	*It will help if I practice slowing down my thinking and staying in the present.* *I can think of driving from one exit to the next, giving myself permission to get off at any time.*
What if I miss the off-ramp?	I can just go to the next exit.	
What if the car breaks down and I get stranded?	I'll do the best I can to take care of myself. I can get help if necessary.	*I will try to practice allowing the anxiety to be there.*

It was quite a while before I was able to drive alone. Just months before my first panic attack I had bought myself a new car. Now it sat in the driveway while I depended on friends to drive me back and forth to work. Those were terrifying days! When I was able to get out on my own, I practiced driving my car around the block. Gradually I was able to drive farther, until eventually I could drive within the city limits. However, I could only travel on well-planned routes where I knew I could get to a telephone and call for help if necessary. It was a while longer before I was able to get on the expressway. Just driving near one gave me the shivers. This didn't surprise me, since it was on the expressway that I had one of my first panic attacks. The memory is still vivid.

I remember the first time I finally took the risk of driving alone on the expressway. It was a spur-of-the-moment decision to try it, and I was really scared. There was very little traffic at that time of day. As I entered the ramp my heart was in my throat. My plan was to go only as far as the next exit and get off. Once on the expressway, I had all I could do to keep from flooring the accelerator and rushing to the next exit, which at that point seemed so far away. I just wanted to get it over with. But I drove in the far-right lane and took my time. *The most difficult part was staying in the present and not mentally rushing ahead. I did experience some anxiety, but reassured myself that I could pull over at any time. After I pulled off the exit ramp I sat alongside of the road and collected my thoughts. It was a real victory! That experience was followed by many similar practice sessions. Over a period of time I was able to add more exits, always giving myself permission to get off the expressway at any time. Being on the expressway, whether alone or with someone, was one of the last things that I was able to do comfortably. Now I can drive anywhere, even by myself. The road to freedom is a long one, but it's out there.*

—RHONDA

Taking a Trip

Traveling is usually one of the last things on our list of accomplishments. We seem to have all we can do to manage our anxiety and panic attacks in our own neighborhood. The thought of putting ourselves in a situation where we could possibly experience a panic attack far from home is frightening. However, by starting out slowly (going short distances), we can eventually travel once again.

Anticipatory Anxiety

The What-Ifs	The So-Be-Its	Other Helpful Strategies
What if I can't go?	I still have the option of staying home. Either way I'll be dealing with feelings as a result of my decision.	At first, I could practice taking short trips close to home.
What if I get there and can't get back when I want to?	That's a scary thought, but it is only a thought. Even if I were to feel stranded, I would eventually get back.	I'll allow myself to visualize the worst that could happen and what I might do to get through it, or I could try to be receptive to images of coping well.
What if I get halfway there and can't go any farther?	I could turn back at any time. In the meantime, I'll try to be in touch with the excitement of being where I am.	I could give myself the option of dealing with it at the time.
		I'll try to keep my expectations low about how well I'll do.

On the Trip

The What-Ifs	The So-Be-Its	Other Helpful Strategies
What if I panic?	I'll just have a panic attack. I'm not in any danger.	I can divide the trip up into miles, hours, days, etc., taking it one step at a time.

The What-Ifs	*The So-Be-Its*	*Other Helpful Strategies*
What if I feel anxious while traveling?	The worst that will happen is that I'll feel very uncomfortable. If necessary, I'll get out and walk around.	*It might help to record the trip in a journal. I could keep track of my thoughts and feelings, and perhaps even monitor my anxiety level.*
What if I get ill while I'm away from home?	There's help available wherever I go.	*I can take along a tape that might help me with my self-talk.*
		I can try to see the trip as practice in allowing myself to be anxious while away from home.

Recently I took the risk of traveling. I hadn't traveled for quite a few years, not because I didn't want to go, but because my anxiety stopped me. Even medication didn't help when I went that far from home. Well, about a month ago I had the opportunity to go up north with a friend to see the Vietnam Living Memorial, which is about 150 miles from home. When my friend asked me to go, I hesitated. I thought, Oh-oh, I'm not on medication anymore. What will keep me relaxed? I haven't gone that far in thirteen years. Could my friend help me if I had an anxiety attack? Where would I go? What would I do? *Oh, the frustration of these thoughts.* Finally I thought, I really want to go. I'm going to go and try to use some of the new strategies I've learned. Besides, I do have some new inner dialogue to help me. Go for it! *With my heart beating more quickly now, not from anxiety but from excitement, I told my friend yes.*

When it was time to leave, I allowed for any feelings of anxiety and gave myself permission to turn back at any time during the trip. As usual, I found that the anticipatory anxiety had been worse than the event itself. While my friend drove, I enjoyed all of those small towns that I hadn't seen in years. It was amazing how

I felt. The strange thing was, the farther I got from home, the freer I felt. It was like breaking free of prison walls. I think I felt that if I were to encounter some anxiety, I would be able to get through it because this trip seemed more important to me than any fear of panic or anxiety. For years my anxiety told me where I was going to go and when. My anxiety was my boss. Well, I fired my boss, even though he occasionally wants his job back. Off and on during the trip, it occurred to me, My safety is right here within me. It's not there at home.

—HELEN

FLYING THE UNFRIENDLY SKIES

In the following inner dialogue we discover that the same strategies that work for us on the ground also work in the air: staying with the feelings and lowering our expectations, for example. With repeated practice, the skies do become friendlier.

Anticipatory Anxiety

The What-Ifs	The So-Be-Its	Other Helpful Strategies
What if I lose control and run up and down the aisles screaming?	I'm only having a thought about losing control. Chances are that won't happen.	*I could visit the airport before the day of my flight and watch the planes take off.*
What if I just can't get on the plane at the last minute?	I could still change my mind and decide not to board the plane. Of course, then I'll have to deal with my feelings of disappointment and failure.	*I could plan a short practice flight with a therapist.* *I could listen to a soothing tape for fearful flyers.*
What if it's always going to be like this? Maybe I shouldn't fly if it makes me this anxious.	I can try to allow the anxiety to be there and not try to fix it. Flying will get easier with more practice.	

During the Flight

The What-Ifs	The So-Be-Its	Other Helpful Strategies
What if someone sees me shaking?	They probably won't notice, but if they do I'll try to be okay with that.	*I can arrive at the airport early for my seating assignment so I can choose where I want to sit, or I can arrange that with my travel agent ahead of time.*

The What-Ifs	The So-Be-Its	*Other Helpful Strategies*
Everyone looks so relaxed. What if I'm the only one feeling this way? What's wrong with me?	I don't really know how these people feel. Many of them probably feel the same way I do, and it's okay to feel that way. I can allow the anxiety to be there. There's nothing wrong with me.	*Sitting on an aisle seat toward the front might help make my trip more comfortable.* *I can allow myself to get up and move around the plane once it has leveled off.*
I'm an adult and I'm not supposed to be afraid.	Go ahead and be afraid. It's okay! Everyone has fears, and flying happens to be mine. Actually, a lot of people are afraid of flying. I'm not alone.	
What if I get sick and make a fool of myself? What will people think?	I'll try to allow myself to be sick. People will most likely think I'm suffering from motion sickness.	

I recently took part in a practice flight with a therapist. The trip sounded like a great idea in the planning stage, but when I arrived at the airport, my anxiety was high. My fear of flying had always centered around my safety (or so I had thought). I now realized that I had more concern about how I was going to handle my anxiety while in flight. I thought, What if I get sick or lose control and make a fool of myself? I was afraid of experiencing anxiety so severe that I wouldn't be able to handle it.

During the pre-flight days I was encouraged by my therapist to stay with my fearful thoughts and feelings rather than fight them. Now I was beginning to doubt the effectiveness of this strategy; it seemed like the only thing I was accomplishing was scaring myself. I was about to allow those very same thoughts and feelings soaring 35,000 feet above the ground. I wondered if this could possibly work, since on previous flights I had turned to medication or alcohol to numb those unwanted feelings.

The takeoff and landing were the most challenging parts of the trip. As the aircraft fought gravity, I allowed my anxiety to rise and reminded myself that the 727 we were on was built like a battleship and could withstand the takeoff. Once in the air, my anxiety leveled off. I was surprised to find out that by not fighting the fear and allowing it to be there, I was less anxious than when I tried to numb the feelings or fight them. As a matter of fact, I found myself dealing with the strange feeling that accompanies not being anxious when I think I should be. I felt a wonderful sense of freedom and accomplishment when we landed.

The practice was a success. As it turned out, the anticipatory anxiety had been the worst part of the trip. I also realized that part of my problem was that I have difficulty trusting. Since there was no way I could control the aircraft, I tried to place my trust in people who had been well-trained for their jobs. I congratulated myself for the tremendous courage it had taken for me to make this flight.

—JAN

❦

CONCLUSION

There comes a time in a person's life when he must take himself into his own arms.

—GEORGE BERNARD SHAW

Just as we did when we introduced the book, we would like to leave you with these words: *embrace the fear.* No matter how scary or intense the feelings, that's all they really are—feelings. Rather than trying so hard to get rid of your anxiety, your panic, and your fearful thoughts, you can get acquainted with them and try to accept them.

In *Embracing the Fear*, we are encouraged to become acquainted with our anxiety, our panic attacks, and our fearful thoughts, and we receive the tools to deal with them. As we internalize these new tools and grow stronger, we can acquire more self-confidence to cope with situations that previously seemed unmanageable. The more confidence we have in ourselves and in our coping tools, the better we will cope. This can help us to take the risks that are necessary for our recovery.

We hope that your journey through this book has helped in some way to alleviate your fear of anxiety and panic attacks; we hope too that it has answered some of your questions by giving you new insight into your anxiety problem. Perhaps it has made you more aware of your self-talk and how it affects your anxiety. Perhaps it has given you helpful strategies to work with. For those of you who might have despaired of ever getting well, we hope you will feel encouraged about the possibility of your own recovery once again. Above all, we hope that it has helped you to feel good about yourself and has made it easier for you to be more accepting of your anxiety and panic attacks.

As your A-talk diminishes in strength and your B-talk gains in strength, your problems with anxiety will become less troublesome. Your anxiety and panic attacks will become more manageable and you will avoid fewer and fewer situations. Your catastrophic thoughts will become less alarming. All this will happen slowly—so much so, that you will not even perceive it. But you will know you are making progress because others will remind you of it.

At some point, situations that were impossible will now seem easy, and you will wonder why you used to have any difficulties with them. Your B-talk becomes so internalized that the helpful self-talk becomes your favored way of interpreting and coping with the various aspects of your life.

Recovery needs a great deal of time and patience. It helps if we can give it all the time it needs. May you find comfort in knowing that you are not alone and hope in knowing that there is recovery. And may you find peace with your anxiety through *embracing the fear*.

PART 4

APPENDIX

Although the agony of those early days is behind me and at times seems as though it never existed, it has left me with a desire to give hope and encouragement to those who are still struggling. There is hope and there is help. Above all, there is life beyond agoraphobia.

—JUDY

SOME THOUGHTS ON SELF-CARE*

Because this book focuses primarily on a cognitive approach in dealing with anxiety disorders, relaxation techniques, exercise, and nutrition are not included in our anxiety management program. Although they are beneficial in helping us cope with anxiety, the cognitive aspects of dealing with this problem are paramount: we first need to accept our anxiety before we can do anything about it.

In the early stages of experiencing anxiety and panic attacks, we may be too caught up in the problem itself to use relaxation as the main strategy to manage our anxiety. We perceive what is happening to us as both mysterious and complex. Telling ourselves that we must relax or control our breathing, without first understanding what we are dealing with, can add to our frustration. This is especially true if we find that we aren't making the kind of progress we think we should be, and that in spite of all our efforts we are still panicking. This is understandable, considering our perfectionism and high expectations for immediate results.

Sometime during our process of recovery, however, after we have gained some insight into our anxiety problem and learned some cognitive coping skills, we can practice helpful relaxation techniques, such as diaphragmatic breathing, as another way to deal with anxiety.

Relaxation

Relaxation is a process of letting go, a process that we have great difficulty with, since we are constantly on guard for the next panic attack or anxiety symptoms. This vigilance unconsciously tenses our muscles, especially in the neck and shoulder area. It can also make our breathing rapid and shallow, thereby disturbing its natural rhythm. Physiological changes caused by overbreathing (hyperventilating) can create sensations that resemble anxiety symptoms, such as

---

* The following information is based on author Judith Bemis's personal experience and reading. Its purpose is to raise awareness of the importance of exercise and nutrition in achieving and maintaining better health. Since we all have different needs, it is advisable to check with a physician for individual exercise programs and dietary recommendations.

light-headedness, dizziness, and a feeling of unreality.

As much as we might want to enjoy the benefits of relaxation, it is not something that we can make happen. Trying hard to relax is like trying to control a panic attack. Forcing relaxation can actually create more tension. However, it is possible to learn how to relax, at least in varying degrees, depending on the individual.

It helps to keep in mind that the first step for us in learning how to relax is to allow the anxiety to be there. We only add to our frustration when we try to stop it. When attempting any kind of relaxation program, we are working against greater odds than people without anxiety problems. We need to be patient with ourselves, trying not to feel as though we've failed if we find it difficult to relax or if we aren't making the kind of progress we want. It will help if we think of our practice as something we are doing for ourselves, rather than as the sole answer to our anxiety symptoms or our panic attacks.

Diaphragmatic Breathing

Diaphragmatic breathing can be an effective, calming technique. This is because some of the symptoms of anxiety and panic are caused by physiological changes that result from hyperventilating or holding our breath, both of which affect the levels of oxygen and carbon dioxide in the body. By slowing down our breathing, we reduce our intake of oxygen, bringing the ratio of oxygen to carbon dioxide back into balance. The following diaphragmatic breathing exercise is one that I have found helpful.

Begin by lying down on the floor, feet apart. Place your hands (or a book) on your abdomen, just below the rib cage. Breathe slowly through your nose. Your hands (or book) will rise and fall with each breath as the diaphragm's muscles expand and contract. Think of taking the breath in from the tip of the toes as you inhale, and slowly bring it up to the crown of the head. Pause slightly, then exhale completely, allowing your body to relax. Feel the floor beneath you holding your weight. Continue to inhale and exhale in this manner.

Try not to force the breath or be concerned about breathing the "right way." It is not unusual to hear people say that they get so caught up in how to breathe that it adds to their anxiety. This, of course, defeats the purpose.

The best time to practice diaphragmatic breathing is while resting quietly, not when approaching a ten on the panic scale. Later, after having had some practice, we can apply this technique more effectively in situations where we feel anxious.

Physical Exercise

Not only can physical exercise improve our health and sense of well-being, it can also increase our ability to handle stress. Unfortunately, either we feel that we don't have the time for exercise, or we're just too tired to put forth the effort. It's a catch-22: physical exercise is the one thing that could help our fatigue, yet we're too tired to do it. When we do take the time, however, we find that the rewards are great. Even though we might have started out tired, taking part in some kind of physical exercise can leave us feeling more energized. Aerobic exercise such as brisk walking, jogging, running, swimming, or bicycling can have psychological benefits as well, such as reducing mild depression.

I discovered that taking a water aerobics or dance class was good exercise, as well as a lot of fun. We tend to forget the importance of having fun and the role it plays in alleviating stress. What about those of us who might have a difficult time getting out to a class? Exercise books, videos, and cassette tapes, as well as home exercise equipment, are available. Keep it simple. We might want to consider doing some easy stretching exercises when we first get up in the morning, or taking a walk. Walking is an excellent form of exercise and can be done almost anywhere and at any time. When we are ready to take the risk, we can sign up for a class, knowing that we always have the option of sitting or standing near the door once we get there, or leaving early if necessary.

Some of us might be concerned about experiencing anxiety or panic attacks when doing aerobic exercise. Physical symptoms such as light-headedness or heart palpitations can be disturbing, but the benefits far outweigh any temporary discomfort. If we have a physical problem, or if we are particularly concerned, it is a good idea to check with a doctor to see what type of exercise is best for us.

One alternative to aerobic exercise is yoga. Yoga exercises, with their slow, gentle stretching, are also excellent for relieving tension. Classes are offered in most communities, and books or videotapes are available for home use.

Once we have decided on an exercise program that fits our needs, it is advisable to start out gradually and avoid doing too much at once. It is tempting to rush into an exercise program and overdo it. It's like a crash diet. We eventually get discouraged and give up. We stand a better chance of success if we start out slowly and keep it simple.

Nutrition

Proper diet is essential in maintaining good health, but it is especially important for those of us with anxiety and panic problems, since stress robs our systems of certain vitamins and minerals. We do not need a particular diet, but we need to be aware that while some foods are helpful, others might further contribute to our anxiety symptoms. I discovered that I felt better when I followed a diet that was low in sugar. When we are under stress, our blood sugar level is already elevated. Too much refined sugar only adds to an already stressed system.

Because some panic sufferers are sensitive to caffeine, drinking too much caffeine could also trigger anxiety symptoms. The amount of adrenaline in the bloodstream can double with as little as two or three cups of coffee a day.

Managing Your Anxiety, by Christopher McCullough and Robert Woods Mann, and *The Anxiety and Phobia Workbook*, by Edmund J. Bourne, are excellent sources for information on nutritional guidelines for low stress and anxiety. The authors also discuss vitamin supplements that can be helpful in times of stress.

Changing our eating habits and exercising regularly are not cure-alls for anxiety and panic attacks. But they offer many benefits, and with time and patience they pay off. What we eat *can* make a difference in how we feel. Even though many of us are aware of the benefits of good nutrition and regular exercise, we don't always eat right or take the time to exercise daily. Perhaps because it seems so simple, we don't believe that it could make a difference. If we do so, however, we can feel better both physically and mentally. What a great way to take charge of our lives: taking better care of ourselves. It's good to know that we can make a difference in how we feel.

ORGANIZING AN ANXIETY/PANIC SUPPORT GROUP

Those of us dealing with anxiety and panic attacks can benefit from working together in a group situation. Just knowing that there are others who understand our problems can be very comforting and reassuring. Since it is often difficult to find a support group for people with anxiety disorders, an alternative might be to organize a group ourselves. The question is, where do we begin?

First, we need to decide where and when we want to meet and how often. There are a number of options to consider when it comes to a meeting room: schools, churches, libraries, and community and recreation centers are often available sites. It is possible to arrange for a classroom through community education. One of the advantages is that there usually is no fee. Another is that information about the group can be printed in the community education bulletin. The only drawback is that schools are closed during breaks and summer vacation. Churches and recreation and community centers, on the other hand, are open year-round, but there is often a fee or donation to be considered. A first-floor room, relatively close to the entrance, is desirable for people who are agoraphobic, although this might be a difficult combination to find. However, meeting in private homes is not recommended.

Once we have decided on the time and place for the meeting, we need to contact the local newspaper and community publications. Brochures or letters to mental health clinics will let professionals know that a group is being organized in the area.

Purpose

The purpose of an anxiety/panic support group is threefold: (1) to give support and encouragement to its members, (2) to offer strategies in dealing with the feelings of intense anxiety and panic and the problem of avoidance, and (3) to give others hope in knowing that there is recovery.

Group support helps end the isolation of the anxiety or panic sufferer, who is now able to turn to other group members dealing with the same anxiety problems. Members not only learn coping skills and effective self-talk but also grow in awareness about how their lifestyle affects their stress level and perpetuates their anxiety problem.

But a support group is not a substitute for therapy. Members are encouraged to seek a therapist who specializes in the treatment of anxiety disorders.

Guidelines

No particular format is recommended for an anxiety/panic support group, but there are helpful guidelines that contribute to the success of a group. Although it is sometimes necessary to discuss the problems we often encounter as panic sufferers, it is important not to focus on problems or symptoms during meetings because of the adverse effect it might have on other group members. Getting off the problem and onto the solution gives the group the feeling of moving forward. It is to the advantage of the group to keep the meeting a positive and uplifting experience.

Education is a major component in the recovery from anxiety disorders. Through education comes understanding, which eventually leads to recovery. People with anxiety disorders come to the support group looking for answers for how to deal with anxiety and panic attacks. Having a program provides an educational approach and gives the group some structure. Without structure, the meeting tends to focus on negative group discussion, including (1) focusing excessively on symptoms and medication; (2) focusing on how terrible the anxiety problem is; and (3) dwelling on personal problems. Positive group discussion, on the other hand, encourages (1) coping strategies for dealing with anxiety, (2) effective inner dialogue, and (3) personal risks.

Ground Rules

It is important that the support group do the following:

- encourage confidentiality to build trust within the group
- focus on positive group discussion
- refrain from giving advice
- avoid challenging other group members
- be nonjudgmental
- speak from personal experience only
- share a coping strategy when discussing a symptom
- remember that this is not group therapy

Sample Meeting Format

The following is a sample meeting format used for a ninety minute anxiety/panic support group:

Welcome

OPENING STATEMENT: The purpose of this meeting is to give support, encourage risk-taking, and share strategies for dealing with anxiety and panic attacks. The main focus is on our "Managing Our Anxiety" and "Lifestyle Awareness" programs, which offer the tools we need to help us open the door to recovery. For the sake of confidentiality, anything said in the group stays in the group.

Attendees are allowed to get up and move around, leave the room, or sit outside the circle if necessary. Taking part in the discussion is optional.

GROUP SHARING: Ask members to monitor their anxiety on a scale of one to ten and to tell how the group can be of help. If new members are in attendance, ask experienced members to talk about where they were when they started and where they are now in their recovery.

MANAGING OUR ANXIETY: Read and discuss one of the fourteen strategies from the group handbook, *Embracing the Fear*. Encourage group members to become part of the discussion by asking questions, sharing comments, and so on.

LISTENING TO OUR INNER DIALOGUE: Discuss A-talk and B-talk. Encourage group members to share their own inner dialogue and how it has, or has not, helped them.

LIFESTYLE AWARENESS PROGRAM: Do not overlook the importance of the lifestyle awareness program, since it helps us become aware of what it is that triggers our anxiety and panic attacks.

GROUP SHARING: Discuss risks taken, helpful strategies, concerns, etc. (for example, "The biggest risk I've taken lately is…"). Each respondent is asked to limit comments to five minutes. Speakers might follow this format:

1. Explain the task attempted.
2. Share the anticipatory anxiety and how it was handled.
3. Describe the feeling on completion of the task.

Positive feedback from the group is encouraged.

CLOSING STATEMENT:

> It helps to know that we are not alone,
> that what we have has a name.
>
> It helps to know that this is treatable,
> that we are not in danger,
> and that we carry our safety within us.
>
> It helps to know that this is only a feeling,
> and that this too shall pass.

ANNOUNCEMENTS: Inform members of upcoming events, recent articles, new books, etc.

SOCIAL/LIBRARY TIME: Books and tapes may be checked out of the group library. Members may spend this time getting acquainted or meeting with the facilitator and voicing further questions or concerns.

The meeting format and other printed materials pertaining to the meeting should be made available to group participants prior to each meeting.

End of Meeting

The Facilitator

One of the challenges of organizing a support group, or network of support groups, is finding people to facilitate meetings. A facilitator is necessary to keep the meeting moving in a positive direction. It can be an added advantage to have a facilitator who is recovering from an anxiety disorder; however, people with this problem usually do not want to put themselves in a position where they might feel that they just can't get up and leave. Many, therefore, may be hesitant to make this commitment. They may also have problems with a lack of self-confidence and/or the need to perform perfectly.

One alternative might be to have group members co-facilitate. This helps build their self-confidence and therefore their eventual willingness to lead the group on their own. Facilitator meetings and in-services given by local therapists can provide valuable training for group leaders.

Patience and low expectations are key concepts when it comes to facilitating meetings and organizing social events for people dealing with anxiety and panic problems. Attendance can range anywhere from one to twenty people at any given meeting. And it is not unusual to have a small turnout for social events and seminars, or to have members sign up at the last minute to avoid the anticipatory anxiety brought on by making an advance commitment. We may become discouraged, but it helps to keep in mind that the service we are giving, whether for one or twenty people, is invaluable and that the intrinsic rewards are great.

Funding

Unless we have access to funding, we are limited financially in meeting some of the group's expenses, such as printing and mailing costs, newspaper ads, and library materials. Such needs can be met by donations and fund-raising, however. Other means of financial support could include selling subscriptions for a support group newsletter. Charging a small fee when there is a speaker is recommended.

A Telephone Support System

A telephone support system can be helpful for giving additional support between meetings and for obtaining or giving out information. If it is used as a crisis line, volunteers are needed who can take the calls. Some people in the group might be concerned about becoming anxious themselves when receiving a call from someone in an anxiety state and might therefore wish to refrain from having their number listed.

Guidelines are necessary to make the telephone support system successful. Two important ones are putting a time limit on calls and limiting the number of calls to one person a day. Other guidelines are similar to the ground rules used in the meetings, such as confidentiality, refraining from symptom-swapping, and other negative discussions. Only group members are given a list of phone numbers. It is a good policy to refrain from giving out numbers over the phone to non-group members.

Other Services Made Available Through a Support System

- A speakers forum made up of local therapists
- Annual retreats and/or seminars
- A library of self-help books and tapes
- A local newsletter
- Group practice sessions (riding on the bus together, shopping downtown or at a mall, mini-trips)
- Social activities (movies, picnics, bowling)

Regardless of their choice of treatment, people suffering with anxiety disorders can benefit from the emotional support found within a group. Through regular attendance and the interchange of coping strategies, members experience a feeling of camaraderie, which creates a climate of mutual support and encouragement.

BIBLIOGRAPHY

Alcorn, Randy, and Nancy Alcorn. *Women Under Stress*. Portland, Ore.: Multnomah Press, 1986.

Bourne, Edmund J. *The Anxiety and Phobia Workbook*. Oakland: New Harbinger, 1990.

Hanson, Peter G. *The Joy of Stress*. New York: Andrews, McMeel & Parker, 1986.

McCullough, Christopher J., and Robert Woods Mann. *Managing Your Anxiety*. Los Angeles: Jeremy P. Tarcher, Inc., 1985.

Wilson, R. Reid. *Don't Panic: Taking Control of Anxiety Attacks*. New York: Harper & Row, 1986.

SUGGESTED READING

Goldstein, Alan. *Overcoming Agoraphobia: Conquering Fear of the Outside World*. New York: Penguin Books, 1988.

Handly, Robert, and Pauline Neff. *Anxiety and Panic Attacks: Their Cause and Cure*. New York: Rawson Associates, 1985.

Ross, Jerilyn. *Triumph Over Fear*. New York: Bantam Books, 1994.

Weekes, Claire. *Hope and Help for Your Nerves*. New York: Bantam Books, 1978.

———. *Peace from Nervous Suffering*. New York: Bantam Books, 1978.

INDEX

A-talk, 22, 94
A-talk/B-talk
    balance of, 23, 94
Abandonment, fear of, 6
Absolutism, 8
Abuse, 6
Accepting our limitations, 24
Acrophobia, 5
Agoraphobia, 3
    description of, 4
    serving a useful function, 11
    symptoms of, 4
Alcohol and anxiety disorders, 10
Alcoholism, 6
All-or-nothing thinking, 8
American Psychological Association, 3
Animals, fear of, 5
Anxiety, 3
    allowing, 17
    chronic, 12
    demystifying, 21, 32
    learning about, 61
    managing, 13
    permissive approach to, 13, 33, 79
Anxiety disorder(s)
    acceptance of, 26
    alcohol and, 10
    as a behavioral problem, 5
    being permissive of, 27
    causes of, 5
    denying, 26
    finding humor in, 62
    genetic predisposition to, 5
    learning about, 27, 61
    role of self-talk in, 22
    types of, 3
Anxiety Management Program (see
    managing our anxiety)
Assertiveness, 54
Avoidance, 3, 4
    of difficult situations, 18
    panic-avoidance cycle, 3, 6
    reasons for, 51

B-talk, 22
Bus, strategies for, 119-120

Caffeine, 138
Catastrophic thoughts, 9, 11, 12, 19-20
    allowing, 56-58
Church, strategies for, 96-97
Claustrophobia, 5
Concerts, strategies for, 108-110
Control, 3, 9
    letting go of, 21, 46-50
    loss of, 46
Coping strategies, unhelpful, 6

Danger, deflating, 20, 36, 79
Dentist, strategies for, 98-99
Dependency, 7
Depression, 4
Diaphragmatic breathing, 41, 136
Diet (see nutrition)
Difficult situations (see feared situations)
Driving, 3
    alone, 117-118
    on the expressway, 121-123
Dysfunctional families, 6

Emotions, role of, 7
Environment, role of, 6
Escape/Avoidance behavior, 18
Exercise, 137
Expectations
    keeping low, 21, 66
    raising, 8
    raising vs. lowering, 67-69

Failure
    as opportunity for growth, 25, 72
    being permissive of, 17
Fear
    of abandonment, 6
    of animals, 5
    of being hemmed in, 5
    of dying, 4

of falling, 5
of fear, 4
of going crazy, 4
of heights, 5
of isolation, 7
of rejection, 6
of separation, 7
of specific events, 5
being permissive of, 79
Feared situations, 11
Feelings
allowing, 17, 20, 38-40
denying, 38
expressing, 24, 38
of anxiety, 20, 26 (*see also* anxiety)
need to control, 47
of failure, 8, 25, 72
of impending doom, 3, 26, 57
of inadequacy, 8
of isolation, 88
of panic, 4, 17, 26 (*see also* panic)
of unreality, 4
resisting, 20, 36
repression of, 38
Flexibility, allowing, 81
Flying, strategies for, 127-129

Generalized Anxiety Disorder (GAD), 5

Hair salon, strategies for, 102-103
Health, 4
Heights, fear of, 5
Housebound, 4
Hyperventilating, 135, 136

Impending doom, 3, 26, 57
Inner dialogue, explanation of, 22-23
Inner Dialogue, Listening to
accelerating/slowing down, 42-43
avoidance/exposure, 52-53, 62-63
controlling/letting go, 47-48
distracting/inviting, 57-58
limiting/nonlimiting, 89-90
nonacceptance/acceptance, 27-28,
71-72

nonpermissive/permissive, 32-33, 37-
38, 80-81, 85-86
perfectionism/nonperfectionism, 76-77
raising/lowering expectations, 67-68
Inner strength, 21, 84
Isolation, fear of, 7

Job interview, strategies for, 114-116

Large group events, strategies for, 108-
110
Lifestyle Awareness
explanation of, 23
list of topics, 24-25
Lifestyle Awareness Program
accepting our limitations, 28-30
allowing more flexibility, 81-83
allowing imperfection, 68-69
allowing unwanted thoughts, 58-60
being actively involved, 90-92
being less self-critical, 34-35
being in touch with and expressing
our feelings, 38-40
facing difficult situations, 53-55
giving ourselves freedom to fail, 72-74
letting go of control in our lives, 48-50
living one day at a time, 77-78
low self-esteem, 86-87
slowing down, 43-45
understanding events in our lives,
63-65

Managing Our Anxiety
explanation of the program, 17
list of strategies, 20-21
Managing Our Anxiety (program)
accepting our anxiety disorder, 26-27
accepting setbacks, 70-71
allowing catastrophic thoughts, 56-57
allowing the sensations of anxiety or
panic, 36-37
keeping our expectations low, 66-67
learning and talking about our anxiety disorder, 61-62
letting go of control, 46-47

no longer anticipating the occurrence
of panic attacks, 79-80
nurturing inner dialogue, 31-32
reaching out to others, 88-89
recognizing our inner strength, 84-85
slowing down, 41-42
taking risks, 51-52
taking the time limit out of recovery,
75-76

Nutrition, 138

Panic (*see also* panic attack)
allowing, 17-20, 36-37
feeling of, 3
symptoms, 3, 4
Panic attack(s)
allowing, 79
being permissive of, 80-81
description of, 3
learning about, 61
no longer anticipating, 79-80
recurring, 4
symptoms of, 4
Panic disorder
with agoraphobia, 4
without agoraphobia, 4
Panic-avoidance cycle, 3, 6
PDA, 4
perfectionism
need for, 24, 67
role of, 8
Perfectionistic strategies, 8-9
Phobia(s)
simple, 5
social, 4
Practicing a nurturing inner dialogue
explanation of, 31-32
Psychotherapy, 26

Reaching out to others, 21, 88-89
Recovery, 12-13
paradoxes of, 13
removing the time limit, 21, 75-76
Relaxation, 18, 135

Rejection, fear of, 6
Risk-taking, 51

Self-care, 135
Self-confidence, lack of, 9
Self-esteem, 9, 25, 85-87
Self-talk, 22
role of, 7-8
Separation anxiety, 7
Setbacks, 70-74
accepting, 10
Shame, 20
Shopping at the mall
strategies for, 104-105
Slowing down, 9, 20
Social events, strategies for, 111-113
Stress, 6
Sugar, 138
Supermarket, strategies for, 100-101
Support group, 88-89, 140-145
facilitator, 144
format, 142-143
funding, 144
ground rules, 141
guidelines, 141
purpose of, 140

Telephone support system, 144-145
Theater, strategies for, 108-110
Thoughts (*see* catastrophic thoughts)
Time limit on recovery, 21, 75-76
Trapped, feeling of being, 19
Travel, strategies for, 124-126

Unpleasant situations, avoiding or con-
fronting, 24, 51-55

Visualization, 41, 95

Work, dealing with anxiety at, 114-116

Other titles that will interest you...

The Dual Disorders Recovery Book
A Twelve Step Program for Those of Us with Addiction and an Emotional or Psychiatric Illness

Men and women recovering from both addiction and emotional or psychiatric illness share their stories of achieving sobriety and emotional well-being. Professional contributors A. Scott Winter, M.D., Paula Phillips, and Abraham J. Twerski, M.D., discuss the relationship between these two illnesses and how to bring structure into daily living. A wonderful source of strength and hope for those of us living with dual disorders. 250 pp.
Order No. 1500

The Twelve Steps and Dual Disorders
A Framework of Recovery for Those of Us with Addiction and an Emotional or Psychiatric Illness
by Tim Hamilton and Pat Samples

Begin and strengthen your recovery from addiction and an emotional or psychiatric illness with the knowledge and wisdom of the Dual Recovery Anonymous program found in this book. In the tradition of Alcoholics Anonymous, *The Twelve Steps and Dual Disorders* provides an adaptation and discussion of each of the Twelve Steps of Dual Recovery Anonymous. 96 pp.
Order No. 1519

The Dual Disorders Recovery Album
This three-tape audio set provides helpful information to better understand dual disorders. The first tape is a two-part introduction that defines dual disorders and addresses the common reactions to dual recovery. The second tape explores how medication fits into recovery and how to avoid relapse. Tape three offers powerful real-life testimonials from people who are recovering from dual disorders. Three audiotapes, 50 min. each.
Order No. 5674

For price and order information, or a free catalog, please call our Telephone Representatives.

HAZELDEN EDUCATIONAL MATERIALS

1-800-328-9000	1-612-257-4010	1-612-257-1331
(Toll Free. U.S., Canada & the Virgin Islands)	(Outside the U.S. & Canada)	(FAX)

Pleasant Valley Road • P.O. Box 176 • Center City, MN 55012-0176